THE GOOD, THE BAD, AND THE
BARBIE

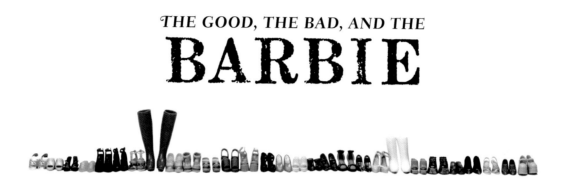

THE GOOD, THE BAD, AND THE
BARBIE®

A Doll's History and Her Impact on Us

by Tanya Lee Stone

VIKING

An Imprint of Penguin Group (USA) Inc.

*For Catherine Frank—who now has Editor Barbie proudly perched on her desk—
and Nancy Brennan. And for Liza.—T. L. S.*

✳ ✳ ✳

VIKING

Published by Penguin Group

Penguin Young Readers Group, 345 Hudson Street, New York, New York 10014, U.S.A.

Penguin Group (Canada), 90 Eglinton Avenue East, Suite 700, Toronto, Ontario, Canada M4P 2Y3

(a division of Pearson Penguin Canada Inc.)

Penguin Books Ltd, 80 Strand, London WC2R 0RL, England

Penguin Ireland, 25 St Stephen's Green, Dublin 2, Ireland (a division of Penguin Books Ltd)

Penguin Group (Australia), 250 Camberwell Road, Camberwell, Victoria 3124, Australia

(a division of Pearson Australia Group Pty Ltd)

Penguin Books India Pvt Ltd, 11 Community Centre, Panchsheel Park, New Delhi – 110 017, India

Penguin Group (NZ), 67 Apollo Drive, Rosedale, North Shore 0632, New Zealand (a division of Pearson New Zealand Ltd.)

Penguin Books (South Africa) (Pty) Ltd, 24 Sturdee Avenue, Rosebank, Johannesburg 2196, South Africa

Penguin Books Ltd, Registered Offices: 80 Strand, London WC2R 0RL, England

First published in 2010 by Viking, a division of Penguin Young Readers Group

1 3 5 7 9 10 8 6 4 2

Text copyright © Tanya Lee Stone, 2010
Complete photo credits appear on page 124.
All rights reserved.

BARBIE is a registered trademark of Mattel, Inc. This book is not authorized by or endorsed by Mattel, Inc.

LIBRARY OF CONGRESS CATALOGING-IN PUBLICATION DATA
Stone, Tanya Lee.
The good, the bad, and the Barbie: a doll's history and her impact on us / by Tanya Lee Stone.
p. cm.
Includes bibliographical references and index.
ISBN 978-0-670-01187-2 (hardcover)
1. Barbie dolls—History. 2. Barbie dolls—Social aspects. I. Title.
NK4894.3.B37S76 2010   688.7'221—dc22   2010007507

Manufactured in China   Set in ITC Century light   Book design by Nancy Brennan

Contents

Foreword

by Meg Cabot

Barbie® Fix

WHEN I WAS SIX, I wanted a Barbie more than I can remember ever wanting anything in my life.

All my friends had one (or more), along with Barbie's camper, convertible, townhouse, horse, her many companions, and, of course, her entire wardrobe.

But when I asked for Barbie for my seventh birthday, my mom just pursed her lips in that way that some mothers do, and said I was "too young" for Barbie.

This was her way of saying she had issues with what she felt were the "negative female stereotypes" Barbie conveyed.

Personally, I didn't see then—and still don't see today—what was so negative about a doll who could, simply with a change of clothes, become whatever the little girl holding her wanted her to be: a veterinarian, a ballet dancer, an astronaut. Or, in my case, a private detective.

My mom's concerns, of course, were more about how Barbie's enormous boobs and tiny waist were going to warp me than about how I was going to dress her. Wouldn't they give me a negative self-image when I grew up? Wouldn't they damage my sense of self-worth? Weren't they demeaning to women?

And so, for my seventh birthday, though I asked for Barbie, I ended up with Barbie's younger sister, Skipper, who had no boobs to speak of, or hips, either. She looked, in fact, just like me. Who wants a doll that looks exactly like herself?

The minute I pulled Skipper out of the box, I wanted to puke.

Don't worry, though. There's a happy ending to this story.

Being as socially backward as I was, I sucked my thumb until well into the second grade. Envisioning the thousands of dollars in orthodontia they were eventually going to have to cough up because of this, my parents were at their wits' end over how to get me to stop.

Finally someone recommended bribery. Mom asked me what it would take to get my thumb out of my mouth.

"That's easy," I answered. "Barbie."

I still remember that trip to Kmart, and my mom commenting on how much nicer all the other dolls there looked compared to Barbie. Was I sure I didn't want a Crissy doll? Or perhaps the Sunshine Family?

Yeah, right.

Once my first Barbie was secured, I kept my end of the bargain: I never sucked my thumb again.

I didn't want to. I had the best fix a girl could have. That Barbie is the most beautiful thing I have ever owned (Quick Curl, with her pearl necklace, and the Ballerina Snowflake Barbie Fairy Costume I bought to go with her). I still have her (in the ballerina costume) to this day, and all the many clothes I purchased for her—with my own money. Supporting my Barbie fix was what started me on a path to eventually becoming a money-hoarding multimillionaire, refusing loans to family members who mistreated or laughed at me and my youthful Barbie dreams. If you think I'm lying about this, just ask my youngest brother.

Of course Barbie was useless without a Ken (in my mind, Ned Nickerson to her Nancy Drew). I saved my birthday money and purchased him myself (Malibu, plastic, painted-on hair). Skipper always played the crazed serial killer who Barbie and Ken hunted down and then prosecuted to the fullest extent of the law.

When Ken lost his arm in a freak dirt-pile accident in my neighbor's backyard, Barbie didn't mind. She still loved him anyway. Because Barbie didn't care about looks. She never did. She'd always existed solely for little girls to project their own fantasies onto.

And maybe that's what had women like my mom so worried. Maybe they looked at Barbie and felt that their daughters would see only those boobs and that waist and forget what their mothers had struggled so long and so hard for. Maybe they would think that the only kind of future they had in store for them was one as the Ballerina Snowflake Fairy.

But our moms needn't have worried. All they had to do was drop by for a game of Barbies at my house.

Then they could have seen what I saw: that my friend Erika always wanted her Barbie to be an actress. Now Erika is a commercial voice-over actress.

Or that my friend Natalie always wanted her Barbie to be a teacher. In real life, my friend Natalie is a literature professor at a prestigious university.

Or that my friend Sarah always made her Barbie rush around, helping all the other Barbies' pets to give birth. Today, Sarah runs the Humane Society in my hometown.

And me? Yeah, my Barbie was always solving crimes—those incredibly elaborate, intricate mysteries that I used to stay up nights writing in my head, so my friends and I, and their Barbies, could act them out the next day.

The only difference is that now I write those stories down on paper, instead of acting them out with dolls.

How Barbie looked was never the issue. Not to the girls who loved her. It was what she taught us that mattered.

And what she taught us was that, like Barbie, we could be anything we wanted to be.

So that's exactly what we all became.

Prologue

*

Happy Birthday, Barbie!

IT WAS A very pink year. Barbie turned fifty in March 2009, and boy did she ever have a birthday blowout bash. From Mexico City to Paris to Sydney to Shanghai, huge parties were held in her honor all over the world. There were fashion shows and introductions of must-have new dolls and accessories. *Saturday Night Live*'s Kristen Wiig donned a black-and-white zebra-striped bathing suit just like the one the first Barbie wore. Everywhere, it seemed, stories about Barbie were shared, articles published, works of art put on display, and conventions for collectors held. There were tributes galore. In Malibu, California, atop a cliff overlooking the ocean, the hottest and hippest celebrities celebrated her birthday in style at a life-size, 3,500-square-foot Dream House created for the momentous occasion by famous interior designer Jonathan Adler.

One of her most glamorous birthday galas was held on Valentine's Day in New York City during Fashion Week, with fifty designers putting on an all-Barbie runway show with fifty-one live models (including one Ken). Fashion designer Peter Som summed up the prevailing mood that night: "Barbie really means you can do anything. You can be glamorous, you can have a fabulous career. You can have a grand house. And you can do whatever you want. She's the American Dream." Anyone who wanted to celebrate Barbie's birthday had plenty of opportunities to have a blast.

But those who do not adore the bombshell babe either ignored her milestone birthday or added their voices to the chorus of people who feel that Barbie negatively affects girls. Striving to be perfect is a stressful goal that can lead to misery, and there are many who attribute this affliction to the doll.

Consider the comments of renowned psychiatrist Dr. Carole Lieberman, who is an expert both on body image and on how the media affects our minds. She writes, "Barbie has been the #1 most destructive force on the self-image of women all over the globe! Little girls, given Barbies, grow up believing that they are not pretty enough or lovable enough because they do not look like her!" Dr. Lieberman is certainly not alone in this opinion. Seven-year-old Eliza wrote, "I could search the whole world and not find a because my mom never had any when she was younger. She used me as an excuse so she could play with them. I would deliberately get them out and mess up their perfectly organized boxes."

**"She's the American Dream."
—Peter Som, designer**

Meanwhile, Barbie does not upset others at all. They believe Barbie is simply a doll, not a cause of the problems with which girls grapple. Kate says, "My sister and I never once considered what Barbie looked like or what the 'ideal' body type was. For us, it was entirely about the clothes!" And Ann-Marie writes, "I never once admired her body. . . . I was surprised later in life to discover that there were women who grew up thinking that

"Barbie has been the #1 most destructive force on the self-image of women all over the globe!" —Dr. Carole Lieberman, psychiatrist

person who looks like her." Emotions can run high. Fourteen-year-old Brooke remembered, "When I was younger, I had many Barbies. Truthfully, I hated them. The only reason I had so many was Barbie was supposed to represent the 'perfect' female body."

There are still others who believe the doll helps women evolve in a positive way. They see her as a symbol of empowerment.

On the occasion of Barbie's birthday, M. G. Lord, author of *Forever Barbie*, said, "I think Barbie really was in a lot of ways the first feminist. She kind of pointed the way out of the kitchen for little girls." And Ruth Handler herself—the inventor of Barbie and founding mother of her maker, Mattel—said, "Barbie has always represented the fact that a woman has *choices*."

Barbie is arguably the most famous doll in the world. She has stepped into the always-fashionable shoes of more than one hundred twenty careers, which

> **"Barbie has always represented the fact that a woman has *choices*."**
> **—Ruth Handler**

include her being an independent candidate for president four times, an astronaut several times, a surgeon, an Olympic gold medalist, and a U.S. Air Force pilot. She has represented fifty different nationalities. In America, girls between the ages of three and six own an average of twelve Barbie dolls, and 90 percent of girls between the ages of three and ten own at least one. And somewhere in the world, according to Mattel, a Barbie doll is purchased every three seconds.

To find out why, let's go back to her roots, and to the woman who made her a star.

This Barbie ran for president in 2008.

The Moment of Ruth

RUTH HANDLER LOOKED absolutely nothing like a Barbie doll. And she did not aspire to. A self-proclaimed tomboy, Ruth was confident, self-assured, and ambitious. She was born Ruth Mosko on November 4, 1916, in Denver, Colorado. Ruth was her parents' tenth and last child—and only the third member of her family to be born in the United States. Her father, Jacob, had emigrated from Poland to America in 1906, and her mother, Ida, and seven of Ruth's siblings followed within two years. Jacob arrived in America at Ellis Island in New York City, but moved west to Denver, where there was a Jewish community that rivaled the size of that in Manhattan. He was a large man who was tough but well liked, and a hard worker. Jacob started a business making bodies for trucks. Although he was a skilled businessman, he was also a gambler, and the family was often short on money. Ruth's older siblings had to pitch in and never received the kind of education that Ruth and some of the other Mosko siblings did. And for some of them, the gambling behaviors of their father rubbed off and stuck with them for life. But for Ruth, it was something else that changed her life forever.

When Ruth was just six months old, her mother, Ida, had to have surgery. To help out, Ruth's older sister Sarah took Ruth in. Sarah was twenty years old at the time and had recently married Louis Greenwald. At first, Ruth's living with Sarah was just a temporary arrangement, but the surgery left Ida weak, and having Sarah continue to help with the baby seemed to make sense to all involved. Ruth never went back to her parents' house and instead was raised about a mile away. The two families saw each other for Friday night dinners at the Mosko house but led fairly separate lives. They attended different synagogues and Ruth went to a different school from her brothers and sisters. In addition, her siblings knew Yiddish, the main language of their parents, but English was the language spoken in the Greenwald home. So when Ruth did spend time with her parents, it was difficult for them to communicate with each other.

As an adult, Ruth was annoyed by people saying that her mother abandoned her and implying that this influenced the ambitious person she became. Ruth said in her autobiography, "It has been suggested to me once or twice that this supposed 'rejection' by my mother may have been what spurred me to become the kind of person who always has to prove

herself. This seems like utter nonsense to me." But she did recognize that trait in herself, as she also said, "I guess I've had this overwhelming compulsion to prove myself all my life." Ruth never did put her finger on the source of that feeling, but she did recognize her sister Sarah as "the greatest influence on the woman I was to become."

There is no question that Sarah loved Ruth and treated her like a daughter. Ruth's brother Aaron remembered, "Sarah was just trying to relieve pressure on my mother, but she became attached to Ruth and no way she'd give her back." And when Sarah learned that she was unable to have children, it may have cemented her bond with her baby sister even more firmly.

"[Sarah] was a fantastic role model and I absolutely idolized her. She always worked outside the home, seemed to thrive on working, so I grew up with the idea that a woman—a *mother*—with a job was neither strange nor unnatural."

—Ruth Handler

The fact remains that Ruth grew up with an extended family of strong, supportive people. She called her biological parents Ma and Pa and said, "To me, they seemed more like loving, indulgent grandparents. My most vivid memories of Ma have the kitchen as a backdrop. She was always in there cooking something special for one or another of us." And Sarah and Louis gave Ruth everything she needed—and sometimes more. Although Aaron said she was "treated like a queen," Ruth did not have an entitled attitude. In fact, she seemed to want to work hard either to be worthy of all she had been given, or perhaps to repay a debt that only she felt.

When she was ten, Ruth went to work in the pharmacy that Sarah and Louis had opened. She couldn't wait to get there after school. "I used to love it. I used to wait on trade. I worked the cash register. They had a small soda fountain where I became a 'soda jerk.'" Ruth also loved to be around Sarah, who—although she only had the benefit of a few years of elementary school—was an intelligent and savvy businesswoman as well as a wonderful role model for Ruth. Sarah made sure the business ran smoothly, despite the fact that Louis turned out to have a gambling problem of his own and was not always as responsible as he could have been.

Ruth had *hard worker* written all over her. She had friends and liked spending time with them, but even as a young teen, as she noted in her autobiography, she "simply preferred working over playing with other kids." She wrote, "It's not

"I didn't like dolls and never played with them." —Ruth Handler

that I *never* played, but I was basically a loner." It is ironic, too, that the woman who would go on to create the most popular doll of all time had no interest in that kind of play as a child. "I didn't like dolls and never played with them. Sarah, on the other hand, adored dolls and was always buying them for me."

In junior high, Ruth worked in her brother Joe's law office after school, typing and doing secretarial work. And when Sarah and Louis opened a luncheonette, Ruth worked there, too. Her father, Jacob, was one of her favorite customers. "My father loved to come to Sarah's lunch

The Moment of Ruth 🐾 11

counter. At home, he always observed the Jewish dietary restrictions (no pork or shellfish, for example), but . . . he always asked us to serve him up some bacon and eggs!" Ruth even had a chance to manage the restaurant on her own once, when Sarah was off on a trip. "I loved every minute of the furious pace of running the place." Being an entrepreneur was in Ruth's blood.

Of course, she was also a typical teenager who valued her social life. When she was sixteen, Ruth met Isadore Elliot Handler, nicknamed Izzy, at a dance. She had actually caught a glimpse of him two weeks earlier, and it was love at first sight. But Sarah did not approve of Ruth's choice. Izzy came from a poor family and Sarah worried about Ruth's future. "They liked him as a person," Ruth later wrote, "but considered him poor husband material because he was a penniless artist."

Ruth was smitten, but practical. She had no intention of being poor. She was also highly influenced by Sarah's opinion, and the more serious Ruth and Izzy became, the more intent Sarah was on breaking them up. After they had been

Isadore (Izzy) Elliot Handler and Ruth Mosko in 1937.

dating for about a year, Sarah decided Ruth should expand her horizons by going to California to live with their sister Lillian and attending high school there. So Ruth broke up with Izzy and went. But when she returned to Denver, the bond between them was as strong as ever. They were in love—it was as simple as that. After graduating from high school, Izzy was awarded a scholarship to study art at the Denver Art Institute, and Ruth went to the University of Denver while maintaining a job. Work was a constant, college was a given, and Ruth's ambitions were high. This was quite atypical for a young woman in the 1930s, but it suited her well.

Then another trip to California for a vacation almost pulled the couple apart once again, which thrilled Sarah. "Cross your fingers," she told one of her sisters. "With any luck she'll meet a doctor, lawyer, or businessman out there and forget about Izzy once and for all!" It might have turned out that way, because Ruth ended up staying in California—and for a reason that speaks volumes about the kind of motivated, can-do person she was. One day, Ruth had lunch with a woman who was a friend of the family. The woman

"Though I really hadn't been interested in pursuing such a job myself [at the Studios at Paramount], that word 'impossible'—even way back then—turned the idea into an irresistible challenge." —Ruth Handler

worked at Paramount, a famous movie studio. Ruth was intrigued by the atmosphere and asked how a person might get a job at a movie studio. When the woman told her it was practically impossible, that was all Ruth needed to hear. In no time, she had arranged for an appointment at the hiring office and talked her way into a job at Paramount!

So Ruth was in California and Izzy

"WHILE OUT FOR my first solo cruise downtown in [my] birthday convertible, I spotted Leonard Phillips, a boy I knew, walking down Welton Street. . . . I had no interest in him, but I craned my neck to get a good look at the guy he was walking with. This other boy was almost a head taller than Leonard, but what really caught my eye was his massive head of black curls. I said aloud to myself, 'Who is *that* interesting-looking guy?' . . . I decided that Isadore Elliot Handler—whose name I wouldn't learn for two weeks—was *gorgeous*." —Ruth Handler

was in Denver—until he showed up at her door because he missed her so much.

Izzy rented a room near Ruth's apartment and they began dating again. After about a year, Sarah went to Los Angeles and convinced Ruth that she was not on the right path and would end up with a poor artist for a husband if she stayed with Izzy. As fiercely independent as Ruth was, she was also a dutiful sister. Ruth gave up her job and apartment, left Izzy in California, and moved back to Denver. But Sarah had underestimated the love Izzy and Ruth had for each other. The two ultimately decided to get married, and when Izzy returned to Denver, Sarah and Louis threw them a beautiful wedding. They were married on June 26, 1939, almost six years after they first fell in love. It would not be the last time they beat the odds—together.

2

The Making of Mattel

THE NEWLYWEDS WENT back to Los Angeles soon after their wedding. They knew they had a bright future there. Now that they were married, Ruth confided in her husband that she much preferred his middle name. From then on, Izzy was known as Elliot. Elliot studied art at the Art Center College of Design and they returned to their old jobs—Ruth at Paramount and Elliot at the Beranek and Erwin Lighting Fixture Company. After spending a few months in a small apartment, Ruth found one with more space, even though it was a stretch to afford it.

In their new Hollywood apartment, they shared a two-car garage with a neighbor, and Elliot turned their half into studio space to make his artwork. At the Art Center, one of Elliot's teachers asked his students to experiment with designing household items using a new material called Plexiglas. Made of plastic but looking like glass, it was mainly used by the military for replacing glass in things like airplane windshields. Elliot looked around their barely furnished apartment and ideas began to take shape.

When Ruth saw his sketches, the entrepreneurial spirit she had developed early on kicked into overdrive. "He was poor and wanted to be an artist," she said. "I didn't want to live poor. . . . We were in a new apartment with no furniture and he started designing stuff for our apartment, and I said, 'Hey if you can make stuff that beautiful, I can sell it.'" With no sales experience, and armed only with her confidence in Elliot's designs and her natural inclination to take risks,

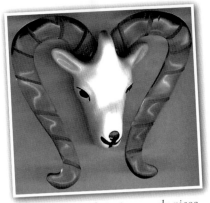

This ram's head pin is an early piece of Elzac jewelry.

Ruth convinced Elliot to quit his job and set up shop in the garage. When the dust and clutter caused problems with their neighbor, they scraped their pennies together and rented two hundred square feet of space and turned that into a studio. They were one step closer to creating a successful business.

Elliot made bookends, trays, mirrors, and other accessories in their workshop while Ruth kept working at Paramount. After work and during lunch hours she made sales calls and marketed Elliot's designs. It wasn't long before their efforts paid off. With orders to fill, the couple now needed more money to buy materials and get their business off the

"I was fit to be tied with staying home. I hated it. I couldn't stand it. It was awful."
—Ruth Handler

ground. Elliot's brother Al and Ruth's sister Sarah both lent them money, as did a few friends and other family members. And an old coworker of Elliot's, Harold "Matt" Matson, came to work with them. Elliot's talents extended beyond his designs; he also had a knack for knowing what people wanted to buy. He started to make jewelry and furniture as well, which sold to stores easily. In the meantime, Ruth left her job at Paramount. Soon after, she became pregnant, and Barbara Joyce Handler was born on May 21, 1941. Nearly three years later, on March 22, 1944, Ruth had a baby boy—Kenneth Robert, or Ken, as he was called.

Meanwhile, Elliot had continued to do well, going into business with Zachary Zemby and forming a company they named Elzac, which manufactured Elliot's products. Matt Matson worked with them too. Ruth had been staying at home full-time with Barbara and Ken, but she was extremely restless. She wrote, "Though I dearly loved my children . . . and made them my first priority, the staying home part just wasn't in my makeup." She also "missed the fast-paced business world and the adrenaline rush that came with closing a tough sale and delivering a gigantic order on time." Ruth was nearly thirty years ahead of her time—it wasn't until the 1970s that many women sought to combine working full-time outside of the home with being a wife and mother.

It turned out Ruth wasn't the only one who was unhappy. Not long after Ken was born, Elliot and Zemby disagreed about how to run Elzac. Matson, exhausted from working at the factory and running interference between the others, quit. When Ruth heard this, she told Elliot they should meet with him. Upon learning that Matson was still interested in selling Elliot's designs, Ruth had a brainstorm: The three of them should start a new business together. Ruth and Matt had faith that Elliot's instincts were strong. He would design beautiful things, Matson would produce the products, and Ruth would sell them. After they sold their first big order of picture frames, they formed a company. They played around with potential names for it, and ended up agreeing that Ruth's name was too hard to work in. But Matt and Elliot combined well to make Mattel. Little did they know, a toy giant had just been born.

Ruth was seemingly tireless—and bold. The mother of a three-year-old and an infant, she threw herself into work, sometimes with kids in tow. But Sarah and Louis had moved to California to be near them, so Ruth had some help with the children. Even though their company was young and small, she presented herself to potential buyers as though Mattel was a major player. She dressed the part, with tailored suits, and perfect hair and makeup, and made sure there was enough money to buy materials. She even learned how to drive a big truck—at a time when many women didn't even drive cars—to deliver the products herself when needed. "I was frightened and determined . . . [but] I was gutsy. I made it work," she said.

As Mattel grew, it demanded more and more of her time. Motherhood often took a backseat, which was a source of friction

Ruth and Elliot Handler, with their children, Ken and Barbara.

different," Barbara later said. Ruth tried to find a balance, but admitted that it was difficult. "When it came to being a good mother, those things like knowing how to cook and keeping a good house and spending the time with my children and all that, I was not really a very good mother, because I had so much on my mind that it was hard to fit it all in." As driven as Ruth was, the strained relationship between her and Barbara was tough on both of them.

Elliot and Ruth, though, made an impressive team. When Elliot started making dollhouse furniture from scraps of leftover materials, Ruth encouraged him to make a whole line. Their combined instincts were a recipe for success. Mattel made a nice profit its first year with the sales of Elliot's doll furniture. Next, Elliot designed a toy bank, a play makeup kit, and a toy ukulele called a Uke-A-Doodle. Around this time, Matson decided he wanted out of the company. It was too

between Ruth and her daughter. They did spend time together, but Barbara wanted her mother to be like her friends' moms who were home after school and cooked dinner for the family. That just wasn't Ruth. She was always working. "Oh, how I hated my mother being in business when I was young, and even when I was a teenager. . . . I kept wondering why we were so

stressful a lifestyle for him, and he and Ruth didn't get along very well. Louis, Sarah's husband, paid Matson the $10,000 he had invested in the company, plus another $5,000. Now Louis was Ruths and Elliot's partner.

Mattel grew by leaps and bounds. Elliot's creative impulses were whimsical and led him to design things like costume jewelry and children's playthings. That suited Ruth's business sense just fine. It was 1946—World War II was over, there was a baby boom, and toys were in demand. And her husband had a unique talent. She later said, "He was, unquestionably, the best toy designer in the entire world." But it was not all smooth sailing. When a rival made a knockoff of one of their early toys, Ruth

"Yes, it was Elliot's designs. Yes, it was Elliot's name. Yes, he was very much a part of it in my mind. But I actually started Mattel." —Ruth Handler

side of Ruth. By 1952, the company, with headquarters in Hawthorne, California, employed seven hundred factory and office workers, and although Ruth was known for being extremely tough, the Handlers did their best to create a family atmosphere. "We knew every single person," Ruth said. "We knew their names and they knew us. We had a lot of group events and we had a lot of fun." They also

"I was gutsy. I made it work." —Ruth Handler

sued. She didn't care that the amount of money she won didn't do more than cover her legal fees. She was sending a message that nobody was going to take advantage of Mattel.

Most of Mattel's employees at the time, however, saw a much different

donated money to charity, as well as toys to kids in need. There was something else strikingly different about Mattel. It was a diverse and open workplace from its earliest days.

The bulk of the people working on the production lines were women, and there were people of different ethnicities working together too—something quite uncommon in the early 1950s. Their first head of production was an African American man named Paul Blair. The Handlers had a simple philosophy: hire the best person for each job. They didn't think much further than that. "It's not that we intentionally set out to integrate our plant, it just never occurred to us to worry about such things," Ruth wrote. "It was unheard of in those days to put a black production worker next to a white production worker and have them all share toilet facilities." In 1951,

The Mickey Mouse Club was one of the first television shows just for kids.

the Urban League recognized Mattel for its hiring practices. And a letter from the Los Angeles Conference on Community Relations stated, "A tour of your plant is like walking through the United Nations. . . . People of different races, various religious faiths, handicapped people, elderly people, all working as a unit. You have set an example that might well be followed by businesspeople everywhere." Their employees appreciated the Handlers as well. One female worker wrote, "I know that my life has been enriched by working here. . . . I have learned through *experience* that working with races other than my own . . . that all have their own individual gifts and that we are all the same after all—Americans."

What happened next for the company really made Mattel a household name. Elliot's new toy, the Burp Gun, was a shiny, rapid-fire cap gun that looked real and even smoked after it was fired. The year was 1955, and wWalt Disney had just opened a theme park called Disneyland. He had also created a new television show just for kids, called *The Mickey Mouse Club*, which was about to begin airing. Few television shows had been targeted specifically at children before, which meant ads for kid-friendly products like toys or candy were rare. When they did air, it was only during the season leading up to Christmas. Toys were advertised mainly in store catalogs, with ads directed at parents, not kids.

But Disney had a new show and Mattel had a new toy, and the face of advertising was about to dramatically change. The show was to air on the ABC network. Disney wanted advertisers to make a year-round commitment to *The Mickey Mouse Club*, and promise not to cancel their contract. ABC was confident that the exposure would pay off for a toy company with the vision and the guts to take a risk, and thought Mattel might be that company. It was an idea tailor-made to excite Ruth Handler. The price for a year-round ad spot was $500,000—the entire net worth of Mattel. She and Elliot asked the head of Mattel's finances, Yasuo Yoshida, what would happen if the gamble didn't pay off. Would they be out of business? "I don't think you would be broke," he answered. "I think you would be badly bent." That was all Ruth needed to hear.

"BY THE DAY before Christmas, there wasn't a Burp Gun to be found anywhere at Mattel except for two defective ones. Even they didn't last long. One of our engineers repaired them and sent them on their way—the first to the White House so as not to disappoint a young grandson named David Eisenhower and the other to a San Francisco newspaper columnist who had promised a Burp Gun to a boy in the hospital."

—Ruth Handler

"It was the easiest sale ABC ever made," she later said.

The relationship had a shaky beginning. The Burp Gun was introduced in March at Toy Fair—where companies show their products to store buyers—and it was a hit, exciting the buyers, who placed large orders. But *The Mickey Mouse Club* didn't air until the fall. That meant that Burp Guns filled toy store shelves before consumers—kids and parents— knew anything about the new toy. Stores started canceling their orders because it wasn't selling. "Things got pretty bleak around our place," Ruth said. But after Thanksgiving, once the TV ads had had a chance to air, Ruth said, "It was like the roof was going to blow off the place with excitement." By Christmas, Mattel had sold enough Burp Guns to equal sales of all Mattel toys the year before. Mattel now had proof that marketing directly to kids—instead of to parents and toy store buyers—was a smart way to go. And Ruth knew exactly what toy would appeal to girls.

3
A Star Is Born

THROUGH THE EARLY 1950s, Elliot had been in charge of coming up with new ideas for products. He was the creative force behind Mattel. But Ruth had an idea of her own that had been brewing for a while. She had been paying attention to her daughter's play habits for several years, and one thing she noticed was that Barbara and her friends lost interest in their baby dolls at a young age. And baby dolls made up the bulk of dolls that were available to girls in the 1950s.

These dolls gave little girls an important outlet for playing Mommy and other games that involved nurturing and caring for their babies at home. But not everyone wanted to do that. Writer Amy Goldman Koss remembered there were "those who longed for Easy-Bake Ovens, Betsy Wetsies . . . or Ginny dolls, whose figures were as boring and flat-chested as our own. . . . My group [of friends] was grossed out by babies and dreaded the prospect of motherhood and ovens and houses and cars and all the things that put the 'dull' in adult." Author Susan Shapiro didn't want to play Mommy either. She wrote, "Do you really want to say to a little girl: 'You have to be a mummy to a chubby baby doll.' . . . That's saying you have to be a caretaker. You want to tell a three-year-old that her job is to be a caretaker?" And if girls wanted to act out more grown-up games, imagining their lives as older girls or single women, the baby dolls didn't satisfy that need.

The other category of available dolls was generally referred to as "glamour" dolls. These dolls—such as Little Miss Revlon or the Coty Girl—were often made to encourage girls and women to buy and learn how to use beauty products, some of which were sold with the dolls. Madame Alexander's Cissy doll was the leader of these fashion dolls, with its beautiful clothes. All of these dolls were meant to appear much older than baby dolls, and were often sold with fancy lingerielike undergarments. They also had arched feet, painted nails, makeup, and styled hair, though their bodies and faces were quite childlike.

Ruth's daughter and her friends weren't interested in either of these types of dolls. Instead, they played with adult paper dolls. The young girls spent hours changing the paper dolls' outfits and putting them in all sorts of scenarios. Ruth saw how frustrated they would get with the frailty of the paper dolls and the flimsy paper tabs that attached the clothes to the dolls. "[Barbara and her friends] would sit and carry on conversations, making the dolls real people," Ruth said. "I used to watch that over and over and think: if only we could take this play pattern and three-dimensionalize it, we would have something very special." The timing of her idea was perfect.

It was the 1950s—a time of serious social and political events and also a time in which much of mainstream

Glamour dolls (top) and paper dolls (left) were the main choices before Barbie came along.

America was trying to recapture a sense of normalcy after the tumult of World War II. Homes were affordable and suburban neighborhoods were popping up all over. Items that had once been luxuries—convertible cars, stovetop ovens, and television sets—were now commonplace in middle-class households. Men were once again the backbone of the workforce, coming home after a long day at the office to find dinner ready and waiting for them. Most women who had gone off to work to help the wartime effort had returned to the traditional full-time role of mother and wife. Little girls played at being big girls, and big girls dreamed of handsome young men sweeping them off their feet. The popular culture of the 1950s mirrored all these societal ideals.

Television, movies, and music do a great job of reflecting what is happening in society at any given moment. TV shows of the 1950s that featured typical American middle-class families with mischievous boys and well-behaved girls included *The Adventures of Ozzie and Harriet*, *Father Knows Best*, *Make Room for Daddy*, and *The Donna Reed Show*. Although *The Donna Reed Show* is named for the starring actress, the

The Donna Reed Show, a popular TV program in the '50s, illustrated the traditional family roles men and women were expected to follow.

character's biography does not overstep her boundaries—the mother is noted as having trained as a nurse before getting married and is occasionally shown working as one. And *Father Knows Best*, which began on the radio, originally had a question mark in its title that was dropped when it hit the TV airwaves. Apparently the question had been answered—fathers *did* know best.

In stark contrast to the idyllic family life portrayed in television shows was the wild new music sweeping the nation—rock and roll—that grown-ups were increasingly worried was corrupting America's youth. Elvis Presley, Chuck Berry, and Buddy Holly were hugely popular, prompting kids to freely express themselves through song and dance. *American Bandstand*—a show that featured the hottest new bands and real-life teenagers dancing on the show—became a national phenomenon.

When it came to the ideals of women and beauty in the 1950s, the standards were pinup girls and movie stars. Pinup girls were so named because men literally pinned up their photographs—most often showing these well endowed women in bathing suits—to admire. Blonde, busty actresses Betty Grable and Jayne Mansfield were known for their looks. When the first issue of *Playboy* magazine came out in December 1953, it featured Marilyn Monroe on the cover and as a centerfold. Marilyn wasn't exactly what Ruth had in mind, but all of these factors affected how

she wanted her doll to look.

It would be pretty, but not so specifically pretty that girls could not imagine themselves in its place. It would also have the figure Ruth believed a girl might want to pretend having as a teenager. Ruth thought of her doll as a teenage fashion model, a teeny-tiny mannequin—and mannequins are made with curves to enhance the way clothes hang on them. The doll's wardrobe played a crucial role in Ruth's thinking. She wanted only beautiful, well-made clothes—nothing that might seem cheap or shabby. But when she described this doll with curves to Elliot, he did not see things the same way. "Ruth, no mother is going to buy her daughter a doll with breasts," he said. The designers agreed with Elliot. They also told Ruth that the kind of details she described—a molded doll with painted-on makeup and a couture wardrobe—would be too expensive to produce. It was impossible, they said.

Betty Grable was the ultimate pinup girl.

There was that word again. If a person wanted to dissuade Ruth Handler, the last thing to tell her was that something was impossible. That just egged her on. She was not going to let go of her idea. Several years passed, but as Barbara grew and her interest in paper dolls

> **"Ruth, no mother is going to buy her daughter a doll with breasts."**
> **—Elliot Handler**

didn't fade, neither did Ruth's determination. Then, in 1956 on a family trip to Europe, Ruth spotted a doll in a store window that was a perfect example of what she had imagined. Barbara, although a teenager by now and no longer playing with dolls, even wanted one to display in her room. This was the doll Ruth needed to show the designers at Mattel so they could finally turn her idea into a reality. The doll she saw was the Bild-Lilli doll. It looked strikingly similar to what became the first Barbie doll, although there were differences. Most important, the intended audience for the Lilli doll had nothing to do with kids—it was a sexy novelty gift for men, based on a popular comic strip.

Bild-Lilli, commonly called the Lilli doll, sprang from a character in a comic strip that ran in the German newspaper Bild Zeitung.

Back in Los Angeles, Ruth began researching what kinds of new plastic materials could be used to make the kind of soft-feeling doll she envisioned. She also gave her head of research and design, Jack Ryan, a Lilli doll to take with him on a trip to Japan to see if he could find a manufacturer. Eventually, they found both things, although it took time to figure out the process. There were plenty of

> "We haven't superimposed a culture on the kids. The kids have dictated what their own culture should be. Every commercial was tested with children. And anything that didn't get through the barbed wire on the test never got on the air."
>
> —Cy Schneider, copywriter of the first Barbie commercials

City. First, though, Mattel needed to make sure the marketing was perfectly planned. They knew that parents were going to balk at Barbie's figure. Ruth's main desire was to give girls what she believed they needed—a suitably glamorous doll on which they could impose their dreams. But she knew she had to get past the parents first, and she hired Ernest Dichter to help her. He was a psychologist who had become successful by studying how people reacted to various products and providing companies with advice for how they should market their products.

Dichter interviewed 191 girls and 45 mothers about Barbie. The mothers, as predicted, generally did not like her. One

mistakes as they learned how to mold vinyl in such a way that there were no air bubbles, breakable limbs, or other defects. After many prototypes, Barbie was born. Ruth named the doll after her daughter. Barbara didn't seem to mind—

"I'm sure [my daughter] would like to have one, but I wouldn't buy it."
—concerned mother

except when Ruth would slip and call her daughter Barbie. That was not appreciated at all.

It had been many years since Ruth first had her idea for the Barbie doll, and three since spotting the Lilli doll in Europe, but finally, Barbie was about to debut at the 1959 Toy Fair in New York

mother said, "My daughter would be fascinated. She loves dolls with figures. I don't think I would buy this for that reason. . . . I'm sure she would like to have one, but I wouldn't buy it." Another mother said, "It has too much of a figure." Still another made a remark that could just as easily have been said today: "I don't like the influence on my little girl. If only they would let children remain young a little longer." Some of the girls didn't warm to Barbie either, calling her "snobbish" and "sharp." But the majority of them were hooked. Dichter's true talent was in figuring out how to make a weakness work to a company's advantage. He homed in on the fact that deep down, what mothers wanted was for their daughters to know how to present themselves in a polished way to the world. Dichter said that if Mattel could make the mothers believe Barbie could help girls learn to do that, the company would win them over. So Barbie's full name became Barbie, Teen Age Fashion Model. She was fully accessorized, and little girls could have a field day dressing her. It worked.

Encouraging people to think of Barbie as "real" was also paramount to Mattel's success—cleverly and consciously set up. One of the reasons people still talk about Barbie by name, instead of calling her a doll, is that she was marketed as a real person from the beginning. In her first television commercial, which aired in March 1959, Barbie had costume changes, moved her arms, and seemed to float down the runway.

The first Barbie revolutionized the doll industry. This is a reproduction of the 1959 original, with its box.

Barbie's debut, though, was not on television. Before the first commercials aired, Mattel had to impress the buyers at Toy Fair. Mattel always introduced its new toys at this event, and setting up in the New Yorker Hotel in the winter of 1959, Ruth was buzzing. Nervous and excited, her reputation on the line, her dream was on display. Toy Fair is a bustling make-or-break extravaganza, with thousands of toy buyers on hand to see what the toy makers have come up with to dazzle them. It's when the large retailers place orders with toy companies. Mattel had done stunningly well at

Toy Fair in the past, and needed to hit it out of the park once again. Ruth was so optimistic, she had their Japanese manufacturer making twenty thousand dolls a week to fill the orders she was certain would come in.

The displays were gorgeous, with Barbie center stage at the top of a curved white staircase, poised to sweep down wearing a white wedding gown. Other blonde and brunette Barbie dolls modeled more than twenty different outfits. But something was terribly wrong. One by one the buyers came through—and left. One Mattel salesman later said, "For the most part, the doll was hated. The male buyers thought we were out of our minds because of the breasts, and it was a male-dominated business." Ruth started to worry, but she knew the biggest buyer hadn't arrived yet. He was Lou Kieso, from

A reproduction of a 1959 brunette Barbie ready to get married.

Sears. A large order from him would put Barbie on toy store shelves from Maine to California. But when Kieso did show up, he didn't place an order either. It was a disaster.

"She was very upset," Elliot later remembered. "I didn't think it would be successful, but she did. This was her dream. She put so much effort into pushing it. She did not cry often, but she cried. . . . The doll was like a piece of art for her that held a piece of her heart." Ruth immediately had production cut nearly in half and spent a nerve-wracking spring worrying about the fate of both her Barbies. The doll was in danger of disappearing before it ever caught on. Meanwhile Ruth's real-life Barbie had grown up and was leaving the nest to get married. She had just graduated from high school, and her parents were not thrilled by her decision. But Barbara, like her mother, stuck to her convictions and married Allen Segal. Her parents threw a big wedding, after which the daughter who had

inspired the doll was gone. It was a tough time for Ruth.

And then things changed. It's hard to know whether it simply took time for the public to notice, or if the end of the school year prompted kids to buy toys to play with in their newly found free time, or if some other factor altogether was involved, but suddenly, Barbie was a hit. "When school was out, that doll just disappeared from the stock of the shops," said Barbie's original fashion designer, Charlotte Johnson. "Kids had to have the Barbie doll. . . . It just took off and went wild." The country fell hard for Barbie. Countless young girls started playing with the doll exactly as Ruth had hoped—acting out their own dreams for the future and their own ideas about what it meant to be a girl.

Youth librarian Ann Klein remembers her first doll: "I was the first girl I knew to get a Barbie, and I have very vivid memories of picking out my titillating (pun-intended), exotic, blue-eye-shadowed model with the black ponytail at Hess Brothers

"To first-generation Barbie owners, of which I was one, Barbie was a revelation. She didn't teach us to nurture, like our clinging, dependent Betsy Wetsys and Chatty Cathys. She taught us independence." —M.G. Lord, author of *Forever Barbie*

department store in Allentown, Pennsylvania. Some people rhapsodize about the new vinyl smell of their cars, but I can recall the smell and feel of that plastic doll hair today."

Laura, now in her fifties, says, "My Barbie was an early feminist. She owned the orange convertible and depending on the week, would take either Ken or G.I. Joe for a spin. . . . They were always in the passenger seat—she was in charge and they weren't allowed to drive. . . .

I loved dressing her in business suits and she often wore a hat and carried a briefcase. Today, I am a decorator and I swear those early experiences of putting clothes together helped lead me to this career." Andrea, now fifty-two, says, "As a kid I loved my Barbies. They could take me all the places I wanted to go in the world, without leaving home. For an awkward little only child, she was my glamorous best friend." A nation of girls had fallen in love.

"Kids had to have the Barbie doll. . . . It just took off and went wild."
—Charlotte Johnson, designer

It's All About the Clothes

WITH BARBIE, HIGH fashion was suddenly in reach of everyday girls. Even the box she came in screamed haute couture, with its sketch-pad illustrations of the latest fashions. Ruth's idea worked: Make a teenage fashion doll with clothes sold separately and let girls' imaginations run wild. It was not the doll alone that held such fascination for girls. Just as Ruth had hoped, everyone wanted to dress—and undress—Barbie, collect her clothes, her shoes, and her accessories.

Fashion designer Bettina Liano remembers the doll she had as a girl: "I just wanted her wardrobe. . . . I loved her clothes. I loved how you could buy her outfits on the little hangers." In 2005, Liano designed a clothes collection for Barbie. "I don't take fashion very seriously and Barbie represents the fun you can have being a girl." Martine Assouline, who published a book about Barbie dolls, also has fond memories: "I dressed them all the time. I remember the little shoes. I think Barbie was my first link with fashion. They [Mattel] re-create the most popular fashions of our times."

That is exactly what Mattel does. Through each year, and each decade, outfit after outfit make up a kind of fashion timeline of American culture. Barbie's first outfit was the zebra-striped, black-and-white swimsuit, with the 1950s glamour factor heightened by her white sunglasses and black, open-toe high-heeled shoes. The 1959 fashion issue of *Harper's Bazaar* noted, "The new spring clothes rely increasingly on a lean, defined

(as opposed to pinched) upper torso and waist," and from the beginning Mattel's clothing lines mimicked what was happening in adult fashion. Barbie's first chief designer Charlotte Johnson routinely traveled to Europe to see the new clothing collections being shown by the most famous designers. Johnson's team designed garments inspired by Christian Dior, Yves Saint Laurent, Hubert de Givenchy, and many others. Johnson's clothes were made with the utmost care. Attention to detail was what Ruth had in mind from the start. Beautiful fabrics, minuscule zippers and buttons, careful hemlines,

fur trims, working pockets, real silk and cotton linings, and underclothes. Nothing but the best for Barbie.

The booklet that came with the first Barbie included images of the undergarments a girl could buy for her doll. One woman said, "When you're a young girl, this is all new to you. Dressing your Barbie doll helped you to figure it out; all the private or embarrassing questions found simple and elegant answers at a pace suited to your curiosity." The 1960s saw tailored suits with beautiful jackets, and classic accessories such as pearls, hats, and long gloves, which women wore when dressing up. But Barbie also sported tights and psychedelic fabrics when they came into style. And when miniskirts became trendy, she wore those, too. And

Top: A vintage case filled with haute couture for Barbie. Bottom: This "Career Girl" outfit is the epitome of '60s fashion.

This bubble-cut Barbie (left) is wearing a coat inspired by high fashion.
Twist 'N Turn Barbie (center) and Malibu Barbie (right) show off their signature features.

the shoes! There were open-toe pumps and pointy high heels in a palette of colors inspired by Italian couture, as well as knee-high go-go boots that were all the rage. Even a new hairdo, the bubble cut, reflected the style of the 1960s. When wigs became a fashion staple, Mattel introduced Fashion Queen Barbie, which came with three wigs, each a different color and style.

Barbie's makeup also morphed to match what was hot and drop what was not. The dark eyeliner and red lips on the 1959 doll were updated with paler pinks and peaches in the 1960s. And that wasn't all that changed to keep up with the times. In order to dance to the new hip-

swiveling music of the late 1960s and 1970s, the Twist 'N Turn Barbie with a rotating waist was introduced. Girls could trade in their old dolls for this new, fresh-faced Barbie who could rock out at a dance party better than her stiffer predecessor.

The 1970s brought Living Barbie, who was even more movable than Twist 'N Turn Barbie, letting girls imitate the new images of active women they were seeing in the media. And who better to tell girls all about the best new Barbie than America's sweetheart and wholesome girl next door—Marcia from the hit show *The Brady Bunch*. Maureen McCormick is shown running in a 1970

TV commercial, tumbling, waving, and bending. After each of her poses, Living Barbie strikes the same one, and Maureen exclaims at the end, "Wow! She's real like me!" Girls were wearing bell-bottoms, gaucho pants, and peasant blouses—and so was Barbie. And, of course, there was freewheeling Malibu Barbie with her sun-kissed skin and long blonde hair that became her signature. In 1971, Mattel even gave Barbie a new outlook on life. Instead of the coy, sideways glance she had always had, Barbie's straight-ahead stare was more in keeping with this forward-thinking peace-and-love generation.

SuperStar Barbie was launched in 1977. She had a newly sculpted face with a wide, friendly smile. She was also more glamorous, with a boa, flashy jewelry, and a hot new Corvette, which was the envy of many a girl (and boy). The changes

> "Barbie was her own woman. She could invent herself with a costume change." —M. G. Lord, author of *Forever Barbie*

made to SuperStar Barbie may have made her look less like a doll that every girl could relate to, as Ruth had wanted. But things had changed for Ruth, too. By 1963, Mattel was the largest toy company in the world, thanks in large part to Barbie. In 1967, Ruth was named president and Elliot became chairman and chief executive officer. By the end of the 1960s, the company had become more complex, with multiple divisions, and Ruth was unable to keep the same hands-on focus she was known for. And then, in 1970, she was diagnosed with breast cancer. Many of the details she had so doggedly stayed on top of in the past began to be delegated to others. Her health deteriorated and she became depressed. By 1975, Ruth and Elliot had left Mattel.

Still, true to Ruth's original

The changes in Barbie's face are dramatic—the coy, sideways glance of the original (left) is much different from the straight-on, smiley gaze of SuperStar Barbie (right).

idea, Barbie continued to reflect the changing times. In the 1980s, America experienced a surge of global awareness. Benetton, a clothing company, launched an ad campaign called the United Colors of Benetton, which highlighted the beauty of diversity and of peoples around the world. In 1985, Michael Jackson and Lionel Richie cowrote the song "We Are the World" to raise money for famine relief in Ethiopia, heightening awareness of a global culture as well. And Mattel launched the Barbie Dolls of the World Collection in 1980, with each doll modeling the fashion of the nation she represented.

Girls wanted to collect as many Barbie dolls as they could, and Mattel saw a market for adult collectors too. The 1990s ushered in collectible dolls by famous designers such as Bob Mackie—known for dressing famous entertainers such as Cher, Oprah Winfrey, RuPaul, and Elton John. Mackie had fond memories of Charlotte Johnson's attention to detail with the early Barbie clothes, which eventually became too expensive to make in mass quantities, saying, "Those original Charlotte Johnson garments were beautiful with all those little zippers and buttons. So beautifully made!" Through the

In the Dolls of the World collection, Japan was issued in 1985.

1990s and into the twenty-first century, top fashion designers created exclusive Barbie dolls.

While Barbie has always mirrored what is current in American culture and fashion, the reflection shows mainly a rich and famous person's lifestyle. Journalist Sarah Phelan writes, "Sure, her changing outfits paralleled societal shifts, but as viewed from Mattel's headquarters in Hawthorne, California (birthplace of Marilyn Monroe), that meant a distinctly Hollywoodesque vision." That trend seems to remain true through the first decade of the twenty-first century. Walk down the aisles of any large toy store and the majority of Barbie dolls are wearing things more likely to be seen on celebrities than on everyday girls. But that is in keeping with Barbie's fashion roots.

In the early years of Barbie, while the Mattel designers were creating her haute couture, a whole other undercurrent of garment-making for the doll was happening in people's homes. Lots of little girls whose families could afford to buy a Barbie, but not necessarily to continue buying her endless outfits, had talented seamstresses in their mothers, aunts, and grandmothers. Many women like to sew for fun, and the first Barbie dolls were made at a time when sewing was a staple talent in the household, a skill more commonplace than today.

Actress and chair of the Women in

"You get hooked on one and you have to buy the other. Buy the doll and then you buy the clothes. I know a lot of parents hate us for this, but it's going to be around a long time."

—Elliot Handler

Film Foundation Sharon Lawrence remembers, "My grandmother made elegant and sophisticated outfits for Barbie. Although my grandmother herself was a modest woman who rarely, if ever, wore fancy things, she had a gift with a needle, a great eye, and that Depression-era mentality. While my mom was in high school, Grandma created dazzling outfits right out of *Photoplay* in the '50s, and while I was growing up, Grandma used remnants from those creations to dress my Barbie to a tee. My favorite was a strapless evening gown made of satin and lace from Mom's prom dress. Complete with a sexy side split and bolero jacket, it was a gown even my playmates mothers' coveted!"

Another woman said, "Thinking of Barbie always makes me remember my grandma and all the wonderful outfits she sewed for my dolls. . . . I've saved some of the dolls and the outfits, and they are wonderful reminders of childhood, Barbie, and Grandma!" There are a lot of stories about the bonding effect that Barbie had on people. Many of them were granddaughters connecting with grandmothers. Jane, who was seven when Barbie was introduced, shared this: "I still have [my Barbie] because she reminds me of the special relationship I developed with my grandmother. Grandma was the only one in our family who could sew anything, and she would take scraps of material from her sewing projects and make Barbie new outfits. My parents didn't have the money to outfit Barbie the way I thought she should be adorned, so Grandma was a one-woman haute couture designer (at least in my mind!), and I still get a smile on my face when I think about our time together." And Sally, who loved the handmade clothes her mother made, also remembered the added advantage they provided: "My mother made some of the most beautiful, handmade, knitted Barbie clothes you can imagine. I was the envy of many of my friends. I did use that to my advantage by trading for some of their Barbies' best outfits. I remember getting some of the most elaborate 'store-bought' stuff for free by handing over some of my mom's creations."

Of course, lots of girls felt the homemade clothes didn't carry as much cachet with their friends and were of-

ten a dead giveaway that they were not able to keep up with the costly consumerism that Barbie's lifestyle demanded. "I had a friend whose grandmother sewed her hundreds of matching Barbie outfits," Lise said, but she and her friend "secretly knew they were worthless . . . they didn't come in those plastic packages." For some, even though their handmade clothes were beautiful, it was a daily reminder they could not afford the official outfits. Georgia said, "I didn't want to take Barbie in her homemade clothes around kids who had the store-bought stuff."

Whether kids can afford to buy all the "stuff" that goes along with Barbie is still a dividing issue today. The basic doll itself is reasonably priced, but the clothes, accessories, and bigger items such as houses and

Handmade Barbie clothes, like this sweater, were treasured by some and scoffed at by others.

It's All About the Clothes 39

cars add up quickly. And there is no end to them. There is always another outfit to buy for Barbie. The consumerism related to the doll is over the top, making her accessible mainly to the upper-middle class. Of course, that's what companies do—create a product that is popular and continue to expand upon the things customers can buy for it. But what does it say about materialism? Is having a lot of things supposed to make us happy? One fourteen-year-old had a strong answer. Annie said, "Barbies are a total waste of time and money. They teach kids at a young age to be on the verge of obsessive about 'outfits' and 'accessories' and to waste time on their looks."

With more than one hundred twenty careers though, Barbie needs a lot of different outfits to be properly attired—but sometimes the clothes are questionable. While the 1960s saw Barbie in more stereotypical work roles for women—teacher, stewardess, nurse, and candy striper volunteer—in 1973, Barbie became a surgeon. The good news was that girls had a visual cue to add something other than nurse or candy striper to their ideas of what women could achieve in the medical field. But her outfit

Here are some traditional career outfits from the '60s—Pan Am Stewardess (top), Nurse (middle), and Student Teacher (bottom).

would not play well in the real world. In a scrub dress that fell to the middle of her thigh, with no pants underneath, poor Barbie might get kicked out of the hospital if she showed up in the operating room. The 1987 Doctor Barbie's pink sheath did fall below her knees, and over it she wore a long-sleeve, white (silky and slightly see-through) doctor's coat. This doll was sold with a fancy dress to change into for nighttime activities that would undoubtedly prove to be fabulous. In 1989, Barbie graduated from stewardess to pilot as Flight Time Barbie, although her flight suit was pink and she came with a flouncy, flowered dress in a package that read "Pretty pilot changes into glamorous date!"

Every Barbie outfit has careful attention paid to it, but perhaps for the career dolls this is a double-edged sword. Some feel that Barbie's wardrobe sends the wrong message to girls dreaming of themselves in these professions and that it takes power away from the idea that women are as qualified as men no matter their appearance. Others believe it demonstrates that girls can be as feminine as they like and still be taken seriously at whatever job they choose. It is hard to know what has more impact on girls—Barbie entering "male" careers, or the idea that her clothing keeps her "in her place" as a woman.

In the early 1990s, Mattel's Career Collection, which had the tag line "We Girls Can Do Anything," included firefighter and police officer outfits. As a police officer, Barbie was dressed in a nice navy blue uniform that was fitting for the job, but once again an evening gown was included in the package. Perhaps the dress is there to balance the masculine with the feminine, as in, you can do a man's job and still look like a woman doing it. But some girls may interpret these outfits as a sign that you need to look a certain way in order to be allowed to step into roles previously held only by men. Eleven-year-old Sara cowrote an article about Barbie and commented on the doll's jobs and her appearance: "Although Barbie has important careers, such as President Barbie or Astronaut Barbie, I think people don't really think of Barbie in those ways. . . . The dolls and movies give a different message than Barbie's slogan, 'Be who you wanna be.' The real message is, 'You can be who you wanna be . . . if you're pretty.'"

To her credit, Barbie stepped into the shoes of president eight years before Hillary Clinton ran for that office. And the first time Barbie appeared as an astronaut in 1965, she was reasonably well attired—appropriately dressed for the job and quite fashionable. Not so the next time around, when the 1986 Astronaut Barbie was issued. With her pink, puffy sleeves and knee-high leg coverings, she looked more like an aerobics instructor in space than a real woman filling the role of astronaut. But since the 1965 Barbie had gone into space just four years after the first

male astronauts did and eighteen years before Sally Ride became the first American woman to go into space, perhaps that fashion faux pas can get a pass. Still, it does not go unnoticed. A woman who saw the 1986 version on display at the National Air and Space Museum (NASM) in a "Flight Time Barbie" exhibit commented, "This is an inspiration to children to see Barbie as an astronaut, but I do not think they do her hair like this in space." Another commented, "Why is beauty a central characteristic of an astronaut?" And someone else said, "Real astronauts do not wear hot pink suits."

Here again is evidence that all you have to do is say "Barbie" and a debate will be sparked. The NASM Barbie display showcased the various space and aviation Barbie dolls that have been made over the years. Some people loved it and thought it was a good draw to get kids interested in going to the museum. Others simply thought it was a waste of space. A thirty-eight-year-old woman pointed out that career-themed Barbies are not nearly as available as the other types

"I really love that Barbie can do anything. Our mothers grew up thinking they could be a stewardess. Barbie came along and said, 'You can be the pilot.'"

—Elizabeth Wright

The Good, the Bad, and the BARBIE

Above: Astronaut Barbies exhibited at the National Air and Space Museum. Right: 1965 Astronaut Barbie reproduction.

of Barbies. She commented, "I fail to see the significance of the very few and scant productions of Barbie in 'real world roles and careers.' All the Barbies I've seen on shelves when going to purchase them for my daughter are either scantily clad or 'Cinderella types' waiting for Prince Charming. . . . Take a walk into any toy store and see how easily you can find Barbies offering [or] depicting true career choices." A twenty-year-old woman wrote, "Oh, gee—Flight Barbie? How cute. I especially like the form-fitting uniform that perfectly fits to her exaggerated body. What are this doll's qualifications?" A twenty-one-year-old said, "Appreciate the

gender-flipping roles—Barbie as pilot and Ken as steward, but unfortunately that does not devoid the Barbie doll of its inherently sexist nature."

It is easy to jump on the bandwagon and say that Barbie must be sold as a pilot and not only a stewardess, or a surgeon and not only a nurse, but it's also important to remember that the word *only* can be just as limiting to girls. If a nurse is what you want to be, then a nurse you should be! It is Choice—with a capital *C*—that women have fought to have. It doesn't matter what the choice turns out to be, as long as it is your own.

One choice that today's women have consistently been making is to join the armed services. In the late 1980s and early 1990s, Mattel paid tribute to them with a Barbie for each branch—Army, Navy, Air Force, and Marine Corps. All of the dolls in the Stars 'n Stripes series had African American versions as well as Caucasian. None of these dolls was dressed more glamorously than they would be in real life.

In 2010, Mattel let Barbie fans choose her next career, and a half million voted for her to be a computer engineer.

With all of the many and varied ca-

Above: Barbie's career choices evolved over the years to include a host of jobs that were traditionally male when she was first introduced. Opposite page: Barbie's careers came to include: NASCAR driver (top), Army Officer (center), and Boot Camp inductee (bottom).

reers under Barbie's belt, whether she stands as a forward-thinking role model for girls to be whatever they want to be or a sex symbol putting fashion before function depends on whom you ask. Ruth Handler, as well as countless others, believed Barbie was all about choices and being able to remain feminine while succeeding in a man's world. Others, such as journalist Sarah Haskins, would

disagree. "To my baby boomer mom, and the many moms like her, the marketing drive to present Barbie as a woman with 'choices' was a crock. These were women in a generation that actually made difficult choices about work and family, a generation that knew that real change took a lot more than slipping into a power suit."

5

Plastic Makes Perfect?

WITH HER LONG legs, tiny waist, and large breasts, Barbie does seem to be the envy of many, regardless of how unrealistic she is. Her perfection is a frequent theme with kids and it is swallowed in different ways. One girl said, Barbies "are all perfect [and] it's just too much," while another said, "She is like the perfect person. . . . I don't think Barbie will ever be discontinued because it brings so much joy to so many small kids." These ideas were echoed in dozens of e-mails. Hannah, age fourteen, wrote, "Barbie was never a big inspiration in my life. She was always so perfect. . . . Staring at a beautiful blonde girl, trying to set up another perfect scenario of a life for her was just not my thing." Elizabeth, age fourteen, told me, "Barbie was who I wanted to be when I was little, and who I hope girls growing up today can draw inspiration from." And Jill, age twelve, said, "When I was little, I wanted to be perfect, like all of my Barbies. I realize now that it was a mistake."

Supermodels have embodied a look similar to Barbie's since the 1960s. Thin is hot. Size fourteen, apparently, is not. The emaciated Kate Moss appeared in magazines and on billboards as the sexy ideal in the early 1990s. Thin, leggy, and large-breasted supermodels dominate the fashion scene. Covers of magazines such as *People* are often littered with pictures of gorgeous celebrities who are held to some kind of idealized standard, yet are hounded and ridiculed when they are caught looking the tiniest bit heavier by paparazzi cameras. Fashion magazines frequently feature ways young women can lose weight, make themselves more attractive, and inch closer to that idea of perfection. Sociology professor Sharlene Hesse-Biber writes that women "may never find relief from the Cult of Thinness." And of course there are all the advertisements aimed at women for anything from push-up bras to self-tanners to waxing products. All of these things reinforce our insecurities while

Malibu Barbie epitomizes the "perfect" supermodel look.

preying upon them. As Mary F. Rogers, author of *Barbie Culture*, writes, "Women's dislike of their bodies is thus excellent for business."

It's not as if the picture-perfect models splashed across the pages and touted as the ideal are real. We use computers to airbrush their images and tweak them to perfection, making sure that bumps of cellulite as well as any other visible flaws magically disappear. Today's girls know this; they are extremely savvy when it comes to media literacy. They know about body doubles and Photoshop. Courtney Martin, author of *Perfect Girls, Starving Daughters*, writes, "Unlike our foremothers, we aren't convinced that high heels are made in the devil's workshop or that fashion can't be fun *and* smart." But she adds, "The sum total of all these thin-is-in images *does* have an impact on the way we see our bodies, not because we are impressionable or naive but because we are human." So while supermodel Heidi Klum says she thinks a size zero is a ridiculous concept, she still hopes to "look as good as Barbie" when she turns fifty. We see Barbie-type images of women everywhere—in print, on television, at the movies. The message is ingrained—look like this and life will be fabulous.

But is it always fabulous? Although Barbie comes in multiple hair colors, she is still thought of as the ultimate blonde bombshell—and that categorization can come with a price. "Dumb blonde" jokes abound, celebrities such as Jessica Simpson, Paris Hilton, and Britney Spears—although they have profited from it—seem to revel in their ditzy blondeness despite the criticism they take for it. Barbie had her own moment with the dunce cap on in 1992, when Teen Talk Barbie opened her mouth and blurted out, "Math class is tough" as one of her preprogrammed phrases. When the American Association of University Women took the problem to the toy company, the phrase was deleted, but the damage was done. Mattel's then-president Jill Barad issued an explanation, saying, "We didn't fully consider the potentially negative implications of this phrase."

It is rare for the "perfect blonde" girl to be portrayed as something other than the dumb one or the mean one on television and in the movies. Perhaps that's because we want to believe that beauty is doled out in place of brains, or we're jealous and need to make the beautiful people suffer somehow. This started when women were first put on the screen.

> "Today's media floods us with images of skinny females in tight miniskirts and low-cut shirts, and the queen of these stereotypes is Barbie."
>
> —Sara Newman, age 11

One classic early example was Marilyn Monroe in *Gentlemen Prefer Blondes* in the 1950s (based on a 1925 novel). Year after year, brainless blondes are put in the spotlight. These stereotypical roles continue to pop up in movies such as *The House Bunny*, and in television show characters such as Jenna Maroney in *30 Rock*, Tiffany in *As the Bell Rings*, and Lindsay Fünke in *Arrested Development*.

In the movie *Mean Girls*, both the vindictive and the witless stereotypes appear. The leader of the "plastics"—a nickname that conjures both plastic surgery and plastic dolls—is a gorgeous yet nasty blonde, and one of her followers is a mindless blonde obeying her every command. Media makers always seem to cast Barbie-ish girls in these roles. And yet, Barbie makes no claim to being perfect.

She isn't stuck-up. She doesn't brag about her one-hundred-twenty-plus careers. She's not even a real girl. She's just one example of a massive number of unhealthy ideals our culture puts forth for girls to emulate.

Sometimes the blonde stereotype is turned on its head. The entire premise of the movie *Legally Blonde* is based on proving that someone as golden-haired and buxom as Elle Woods can find her inner intelligence and transform her beauty queen mentality into one of competence if she really gives it a shot. The plot would fall flat without a lead actress who looks like Barbie.

This woman was part of the Miss America protest in 1969.

So if Barbie isn't the only one to blame, why has she been the target of such hatred? Barbie's popularity grew just as the women's movement was taking shape. This meant that as well timed as she was to take off, she was also perfectly primed to take some heat.

In 1963, Betty Friedan wrote a book called *The Feminine Mystique*. This book was a shocking revelation to most, if not all, women who read it. It made the point that women, no matter how much life had seemed to improve after World War II, were stuck in confining roles that placed them as caretakers of everyone but themselves. It had women everywhere asking, "Who am I?" They were determined to find out. In 1966, Friedan cofounded the National Organization for Women (NOW). By 1970, NOW had fifteen thousand members and the women's movement exploded. In 1971, feminist and activist Gloria Steinem cofounded *Ms.* magazine—which focused solely on issues of interest to women—and *Our Bodies, Ourselves* was published by a women's group in Boston to empower women to be knowledgeable about their bodies.

With the momentum of the women's movement, women became more comfortable being outspoken about body-image issues as a public concern. Women protested the Miss America Pageant, and Barbie's body came under attack as many believed the doll's unrealistic shape had a damaging effect on girls. In 1971, NOW included Mattel on a list of ten companies they felt were guilty of having sexist advertising. The following year, the group handed out leaflets at the annual Toy Fair in New York that claimed Barbie and other dolls "perpetuated sexual stereotypes by encouraging little girls to see themselves solely as manniquins [sic], sex objects, or housekeepers." Concerns

one set of measurements has never been decided upon. Depending on how the math is done, these hypothetical measurements can be 27-20-29, 38-18-34, 39-18-33, or 40-18-32. Some do agree that life-size Barbie's measurements are possible, although they are not easily attainable, and only 1 in 100,000 women could achieve them. Others conclude that the measurements are not humanly possible or that Barbie would be too top-heavy or too small-footed to be able to stand.

Writer and feminist Anna Quindlen has been quite outspoken about Barbie. While she acknowledges that Barbie is but one of many examples that hammer us over the head with ideas of bodily perfection, it is clear that she can't stand this doll. In a piece for the *New York Times*, Quindlen wrote about her daughter challenging the fact that their house

"To get rid of Barbie you'd have to drive a silver stake through her plastic heart." —Anna Quindlen, journalist

continue to be voiced today. Several people have calculated what the dimensions of a life-size Barbie would be, although

was a "Barbie-free zone." She told her daughter point-blank, "I hate Barbie. She gives little girls the message that the only thing that's important is being tall and thin and having a big chest and lots of clothes. She's a terrible role model." Quindlen also said, "To get rid of Barbie you'd have to drive a silver stake through her plastic heart."

Yet there are plenty of people who do not see Barbie as such an evil symbol. One woman wrote a response to the *New York Times* the day after Quindlen's article ran: "As one who consumed Barbie in large doses during my 'formative' years, let me come to the doll's defense. I owned more than 20 Barbie dolls in my youth and grew up, nevertheless, to attend Yale Law School and work as a litigator on Wall Street. I strongly disagree that Barbie warped my sense of self." Anna Quindlen's young daughter might side with this woman. When Quindlen railed against the doll and called her a "terrible role model," her daughter replied, "Oh, Mama, don't be silly. She's just a toy."

Like Quindlen, well-known feminist Germaine Greer, author of several books including *The Whole Woman*, also took issue with Barbie. She wrote, "With her nonfunctional body, boasting a nipple-free bosom more than twice the circum-ference of her minute waist, legs twice as long as her torso, and feet so tiny that she cannot stand on them, Barbie is unlikely to have been very effective in her career roles as astronaut, vet, or stewardess." Yet Susan Shapiro calls herself "a raging feminist" and still admits to "being obsessed" with Barbie. "She was beautiful, she had breasts. I think that's healthy. You project anything you want onto it. It's like giving a kid blank paper and a million crayons."

The fact that Barbie's dimensions triggered such strong emotions likely surprised Ruth Handler more than anyone. About the breasts she said, "If she [a girl] was going to do role-playing of what she would be like when she was 16 or 17, it was a little stupid to play with a doll that had a flat chest. So I gave it beautiful breasts." Ruth did not believe that she had created anything close to an unattainable idea of beauty in Barbie. About the first Barbie she said, "I wanted little girls who were not pretty or were too chubby or whatever, I didn't want them to be intimidated by the doll. . . . I thought if she was too pretty . . . they wouldn't feel she was the one with whom they could role-play. So we made her quite bland. . . . We never made her too unachievable." But Handler did go on to address the fact that Barbie's face and shape began to change. "With each passing year, we made her a little prettier . . . and she just kept going up and up in sales and consumer satisfaction. That's more important than adults who had some negative feelings."

Many women recount their stories of Barbie with the predominant memory being the sheer joy of play. Barbie did not make them feel inadequate at all. Sal Kibler, who works for the Atlanta Women's Foundation, wrote, "My relationship with Barbie did not make me feel the need to hate my body. I did lust

Barbie's slim proportions are one of many unrealistic body images bombarding girls.

"Some grown-ups say her unrealistically slender proportions cause girls to be weight-obsessed, though they never say Weebles cause obesity, or Raggedy Ann bad fashion sense."
—*National Review* editors

after her wardrobe, car, and boyfriend Ken." One woman named Stacey, who was heavy as a child, described how Barbie made her feel better about herself when all the other kids wore the latest fashions and she had to settle for outfits "akin to those of the typical middle-aged elementary school teachers." Stacey wrote, "Through Barbie I could live vicariously! Dressing the dolls in all of the latest fashions gave me an opportunity to be and feel stylish. For those hours I sat in the middle of the living room floor dressing, preening, and parading my dolls, I felt beautiful." Writer Laura Ruby recalled, "When I was a kid, I had real women all around me so I never thought I should look like Barbie. Playing with her never made me feel bad because it never occurred to me to compare myself to Barbie."

Girls also share positive stories. This modern group seems to be much less influenced by Barbie's form, able to clearly separate themselves from the plastic perfection of the doll. Sara, seventeen, said, "I never felt intimidated by Barbie or that an identity." Thirteen-year-old Natalie's thoughts echoed these. "Barbie's body never made me feel self-conscious about my body. She is plastic and made to be 'perfect,' but nobody real has a perfect body. I never felt as though I needed to look like her or be like her. I would never want to be like a Barbie. Being yourself is something that's so important, and trying to be something you aren't is ridiculous." Writer and actress Allie Costa said, "I wasn't bothered by the fact that Barbie herself didn't look like me, and I didn't want to look like her. . . . I've always been comfortable in my own skin and have

---

"Barbie's body never made me feel self-conscious about my body."
—Natalie, age 13

I needed to look like her. . . . I never felt like I wanted to be like Barbie. To me, Barbie was a character. She had lots of different looks, even different races, but she was always the singular 'Barbie,' an untouchable thing, not a person who I felt I should emulate. She had lovely possessions and was always portrayed as doing something exciting, but was never remotely human. 'Barbie' doesn't have never tried to look like anyone else. I'm me, and I'm happy I'm me."

Some girls are not only happy with who they are while holding their Barbie, they actually feel bad for Barbie and want to make *her* feel better! It is usually Barbie's impossibly arched feet that bring on this particular brand of empathy. Margaux Lange, who now makes jewelry from Barbie parts, recalls feeling this way as a kid. She said, "I remember distinctly believing that Barbie's feet must be terribly uncomfortable in her high-heeled shoes. 'She would be much happier in a nice pair of flats,' I told myself. So I promptly got out the scissors and chopped the heels off all of her stilettos. Despite the stubby nub on the back of her shoes where the heels used to be, she remained permanently poised on tippy-toe, but I didn't care. In my mind she was infinitely more comfortable; she was much happier." Costa commented on the doll's feet, too: "I'd rather have my crooked dancer feet than Barbie's oddly-shaped-for-tall-shoes feet any day. I'd much rather wear my tap shoes than high heels!"

The outside messages bombarding girls that tell them they are not good enough, thin enough, tall enough, small enough, are so pervasive they creep into our own homes, our own behaviors. Laura Ruby says, "I'm sure my mother telling me I looked chunky had a much bigger impact on me than any skinny doll."

We are sometimes unaware of the things that come out of our mouths that make an impact on the girls in earshot. How often do you hear a woman comment that she looks fat, or put some aspect of her figure down out loud, or remark that a girlfriend looks wonderful—most often equated with thin. "You look so great!" is often followed by "Did you lose weight?" Girls hear every word the adults around them say. They take it all in and it colors their world.

Consider the following real conversation. A playgroup of several women and their young daughters

While some revel in the endless shoes in Barbie's possession, others want to chop off her high heels so Barbie's tortured feet can get some relief.

was gathering. One woman also brought her baby. Another woman commented, "My daughter looked just like that as a baby." The mother said, "What, chunky?" Thus began a five-minute conversation in which the concerned mother was repeat-

<hr />

"I'm sure my mother telling me I looked chunky had a much bigger impact on me than any skinny doll." —Laura Ruby, writer

<hr />

edly reassured by the other women that her baby was simply healthy and that their babies had also been in the "95th percentile" and "turned out just fine." The mother of the "chunky" baby said things like "Oh my gosh, good" and was visibly relieved to hear this comforting news. Meanwhile, a gaggle of girls sat at their feet, soaking it all up. For some of them, the interchange may have marked the beginning of their mind-set about body image.

Girls pay just as close attention to the signals the men in their lives send. Writer and teacher Kathy Chamberlain described her father as someone who "rarely talked, making us unsure what he thought." So when he watched the Miss America Pageant, Kathy and her sisters observed from the couch "to see

what it was that enchanted him." One of her sisters felt that "turning herself into a bathing beauty was her only chance for attention." When one nine-year-old asked her father if she looked fat, he thought it through and asked another dad's opin-ion. He said, "We came to the idea that it was significant that she asked him and not her mother. . . . How he responds to her and reflects back to her is incredibly important."

The research groups that are organized by Mattel also turn up evidence that there are factors in our homes that contribute to stereotyping girls. Barbie historian M. G. Lord was invited to one of these groups in which researchers sit behind a one-way mirror so they can observe children at play without being seen. On this occasion, when Barbie was placed in the driver's seat of a car with Ken as her passenger, a girl in the group grew angry and switched the dolls yelling, "My mommy says men are supposed to drive!" One of the Mattel researchers said, "And they blame it on *us*?"

Yet many girls do report that Barbie played a big part in shaping their ideas of beauty—often leaving them feeling bad about themselves. Fifteen-year-old Luci wrote, "I would love to say I'm confident and don't strive for perfection in the way I look, but if I did I would be lying. Every day I straighten my hair, apply makeup, and put contact lenses in, all in order to feel accepted in my student community, where 99 percent of the time you are judged on how you look against that one girl. You know the one I mean. The human Barbie doll. The girl with perfect looks, figure, and boyfriend. . . . Girls like me shouldn't feel like this, but we feel the pressure in modern society to act and look a certain way. And if we don't, we feel weird or abnormal. Barbie, I hate you!" Another girl said, "Barbie has this perfect body and now every girl is trying to have her body because they are so unhappy with themselves."

Although Barbie is not the sole culprit in chipping away at our self-esteem when it comes to our bodies,

"You never see a fat Barbie. You never see a pregnant Barbie. What about those things? . . . You never, ever . . . think of an abused Barbie." —Asia, age unknown

there have certainly been unfortunate accessories in her past. One of them was in a 1965 "Slumber Party" package that included a miniature scale stuck at 110 pounds and a book titled *How to Lose Weight*. Rule number 1: Don't eat! Yet Ken came with a glass of milk and a bedtime snack. When it was reissued the following year, the scale was removed from the ensemble, but the book remained. When a reproduction of the doll was issued in 2006, a fake book was included to retain the illusion of the complete packaging, but the title was removed, as was the silhouette of Barbie stepping onto a scale.

Many girls are too busy playing with their dolls to consider Barbie's body the same way grown-ups might, but one teenager had a moment of clarity about Barbie's shape when she was little. Felicia wrote, "Barbie comes in only one body type. I noticed this at an early age, when the thought that neither my friends nor I actually resembled one of these beautiful, popular dolls came to mind. I became enthralled with the idea of achieving the look of Barbie: I wanted her clothes, her life, and her fabulous male companion, Ken. I was only six years old, and no six-year-old could ever begin to look like Barbie: with her unrealistic size breasts, her tiny waist, and her clothes that reminded my mother of the teenage girls that lived around the corner. I gave up trying to become Barbie when I realized that it was hopeless."

The professionals disagree about the impact Barbie's figure has on girls, and many have suggested that the doll triggers eating disorders. But it would be more accurate to say Barbie *could* be a trigger for girls already prone to eating disorders. Eating disorders such as anorexia and bulimia are medical diseases. While researchers at the Helsinki University Central Hospital in Finland calculate that Barbie, if real, would be too thin to menstruate—and an inability to menstruate is one of the symptoms of anorexia—they also noted that department store clothing mannequins have been equally thin since the 1950s. Body image expert Janet Treasure said, "The promotion of dolls with such a body shape, and other things like size zero, have wider public health implications, like an increased risk of eating disorders."

Reacting to the notion that many people worry about Barbie's body, psychology professor Ellyn Kaschak said, "I don't think the concerns are overblown at all. Blow her up to normal [human] size, and she'd fall over." (This criticism has

"I don't think [my mother] had anything to worry about. . . . We always knew that Barbie represented an absurd fantasy."

—Sarah Haskins, writer

been postulated by more than one source, and discredited by others.) But Barbara Reid, a therapist who works with eating disorder patients, said that she has never heard a patient blame Barbie. "Barbie is far too voluptuous to appeal to anorexics," she said. And school counselor Debra Danilewitz said about kids, "They have fun with Barbie, but they don't identify with her." She also echoed the idea that it is more likely that the adults in a child's life, through judgmental comments they might make, have a greater impact than any single plaything.

For many boys, a naked Barbie doll may be their first glimpse of what a girl might look like under her clothes. Think of the expectations seeded in their minds. Gregory Maguire, author of *Wicked*, was left with a definite impression of the female form, which prompted later feelings of empathy and sorrow. "The first time I saw a photograph of an actual naked woman with breasts unlike Barbie's, which is to say breasts that didn't meet her belly with the same convex slope with which they left the shoulders, mounds-of-sugar breasts, I shivered for the poor starlet's deformity and wondered how God could be so cruel." Another man, Mark, said,

"Perfect hair. Shapely legs. Faultless breasts. An hourglass torso. For many years this was how I perceived what an ideal woman was supposed to look like. This spurious notion was implanted in my schema at an early age, probably five or six years old. That was when I got my first glimpse of a fully unclothed Barbie doll."

And what about men, as they grow up to be fathers? How do they feel about Barbie's body—are they afraid she will ruin their daughters' self-esteem? One father was adamant that his daughter not be allowed to have the doll because he was worried that "some young girls see Barbie, want her body, and then destroy their own." But when his daughter's grandparents gave her one, things did not turn out to be so dire. To his daughter, it was simply another doll. Perhaps more important, the experience helped him realize that as her father he has "a lot more sway over how she will one day view herself and her body than some stupid doll."

Another example is a story I received from a father and daughter with a strong bond. This dad bypassed any pitfalls from the start, in part by connecting with his daughter and engaging in her play. He wrote, "Barbie was never viewed in terms of some false notion of perfection, but rather a good doll that could be better—and so began the haircuts and colorings, the baths, the skin cleansings, and the plastic surgery." His daughter added, "We also colored her hair with magic markers. I always wanted to change the dolls, because when you get them out of the box, they all look the same: long hair, blue eyes, 11 inches tall. We wanted her to be different, and play a different role in our story than the one that came plastered on the box."

Cynthia Jackson has had multiple surgeries in order to look like Barbie.

Then there are the rare few who *do* want to emulate Barbie, and set out to accomplish that goal. Sarah Burge was dubbed the "real-life Barbie" in the British press. She said, "It's empowering for women to be who they want to be and not just live with the body and face they were born with." About the famous doll, model Irina Creaser said, "She has long legs and a small waist and I definitely strive to look like her. Some people say I really look like Barbie, which is great."

Cynthia Jackson has undergone dozens of surgeries in her quest to look like a real-life Barbie doll. According to Cindy, she was "plain and unpopular," but her sister "was breathtaking. And everyone used to talk to her more and smile at her more and notice her first." When she caught a glimpse of Barbie she saw the potential. "It was powerful," she said. "I thought, 'That's what I want to look like.'" Yet Cindy doesn't attribute her desire to any lack of sense of self. When asked if her decision to look like Barbie was based on any "perception problem in yourself" she replied, "It's not that deep. It's not that psychological." Like Jackson, model Vicki Lee has had multiple surgeries and spends a good deal of her life taking steps to ensure

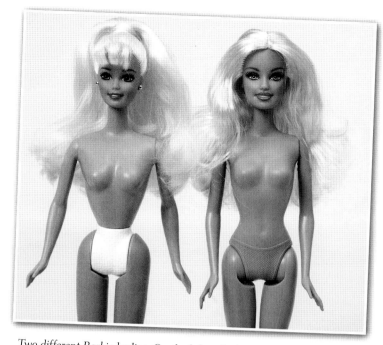

Two different Barbie bodies: On the left is the body commonly used in the '80s and '90s, which was similar to the original Barbie body. On the right is the body commonly used today, nicknamed the "belly button body."

ways glance had gone by the wayside, the "Super-Star" look was born with its wider smile and heavier makeup. It took another twenty years for Barbie's body to be given an adjustment. In 1998, a new Barbie was introduced with smaller breasts, a wider waist, and slimmer hips. Only certain models had these new measurements. Mattel indicated it was the consumers who inspired this change. Girls asked for—and got—a doll that was "more reflective of themselves." But fashion was once again a major motivating factor. Mattel spokesperson Lisa McKendall said, "The fashions teens wear now don't fit properly on our current sculpting."

that she is as Barbie-like as possible. The scary truth is that access to plastic surgery is changing the argument that only 1 in 100,000 women could ever hope to look like Barbie—if they really wanted to, many women could.

Barbie has gone through her own bouts with plastic surgery to her face and her body. Malibu Barbie sported a new skin color for the tan look, as well as a new shade of pale blonde hair. Ten years after the side-

"I think overreacting to Barbie—setting her up as the ultimate negative example—can be just as damaging as positing her as an ideal."

—Abby, age 32

Although some say Barbie is only a doll, it would be fantastic if a toy came along that was equally popular without reinforcing stereotypes. Susan Jane Gilman writes, "Dolls often give children their first lessons in what a society considers valuable—and beautiful. And so I'd like to see dolls that teach little girls something more than fashion-consciousness and self-consciousness. I'd like to see dolls that expand girls' ideas about what is beautiful instead of constricting them." In 2006, when asked how she feels when people criticize Barbie's unrealistic image, Mattel's vice president of Barbie design Cassidy Park said, "I think that Barbie, first of all she's not a human form, she is a toy form. We've never meant her to replicate a real-life human form, so I know the inspiration and the work that's done here to make sure that Barbie can represent so many different things for girls. We take that very seriously and always want her to be a good role model for girls."

Famous feminist Naomi Wolf makes an excellent point that can easily be applied to Barbie in her book *The Beauty Myth*: "The harm of these images is not that they exist, but that they proliferate at the expense of most other images and stories of female heroines. . . . If the icon of the anorexic fashion model were one flat image out of a full spectrum in which young girls could find a thousand wild and tantalizing visions of possible futures, that icon would not have the power to hurt them."

It's Not Black and White

AS BARBIE WAS becoming an icon, the nation was transforming from a severely segregated society into one that started to recognize its multicultural makeup in positive ways. Barbie was created when the civil rights movement was taking shape. She came out three years after Martin Luther King Jr. organized the bus boycott by black passengers in Montgomery, Alabama, to protest segregation and four years before King's "I Have a Dream" speech. Mattel could not ignore this shift.

The company paid close attention to people's desire to celebrate diversity. Mattel also recognized that as the black middle class was growing, so was its spending power. But while the dolls of color that Mattel created have pleased some, they have also upset many who do not see themselves in these Barbies. This is understandable, as there is no more one typical representation of an African American, Hispanic, Middle Eastern, Native American, or Asian girl than there is one of a Caucasian girl. The original Barbie certainly doesn't reflect all white girls. Girls come in too many shapes, sizes, and shades for that to ever happen.

The slogan "black is beautiful" was a clarion call in the 1960s—a phrase that cried out to African Americans to embrace their natural beauty and resist the cultural pressure to try to achieve a perceived "white" ideal of beauty. The stunning Naomi Sims embodied the "black is beautiful" concept when she graced the cover of the November

LIFE

Black Models Take Center Stage

Top fashion model Naomi Sims

OCTOBER 17 · 1969

Above: Naomi Sims changed the face of modeling for women of color. Right: Colored Francie was a step in the right direction, but her name did her more harm than good.

1968 *Ladies' Home Journal* and went on to become the first black supermodel. Before Sims's success, many agencies turned down any models who weren't white. And photographers and makeup artists were ill equipped to find the right cosmetic tones and lighting to enhance skin that wasn't Caucasian.

That same year, Elliot Handler lent both his company's expertise and $150,000 to Shindana Toys. Shindana, run by African Americans, was a non-profit company that made multicultural dolls. Its goal was to make "Brother and Sister dolls made by brothers and sisters." It wanted to provide satisfying ethnic dolls for a market that had few. Shindana did well with some of its dolls, such as Baby Nancy, "a doll with authentic black features and a kinky 'natural'" hairstyle. While Mattel was helping Shindana—which means *competitor* in Swahili—it was also developing its own multicultural doll.

Mattel's first black Barbie doll was, in fact, not a Barbie. Colored Francie came out in 1967 and was a black version of the previously released Francie doll. They were both marketed as Barbie's younger cousins, but Colored Francie was a flop. Perhaps it was the term *colored*, which was already outdated and most likely offensive to many, especially in the midst of the civil rights movement. It's also possible that the fact that she was supposed to be Barbie's cousin made people who were struggling with the idea of integration and interracial marriage uncomfortable.

A year later, though, the black Christie doll was a major improvement. She was sold as Barbie's friend, not her cousin. In the television ad that aired, a white girl was shown playing with a white Barbie, while a black girl played with Christie. Although that seemed to imply that girls should stick to playing with dolls that represent their own race, Christie was still "a daring, big step forward," according to an article in *Barbie Bazaar* magazine. And the idea of Barbie having a black friend made a big impact on many. Journalist Susan Howard said, "You don't know how much it meant to me that Barbie had a friend like Christie. Because that meant, well, Barbie likes black people. And it may sound silly, but it was important for me to know that Barbie liked someone like me. The proof was in her 'designated friend.'" Christie was a big seller. Barbie had other black friends, as well—Cara and Julia. Julia was based on a character from a hit show of the same name, played by actress Diahann Carroll, who modeled for the doll. And since Barbie had Ken, it was only fair for some of the other girls to have boyfriends. Brad, Christie's African American boyfriend, came out in 1970. Cara's boyfriend, Curtis, appeared five years later.

Top: African American Sunsational Malibu Ken debuted in 1982. Bottom: The Twist 'N Turn dolls of the '70s included Christie, a welcome addition to Barbie's friends.

In 1980, Mattel introduced black and Hispanic dolls with an important new distinction: these were not friends of Barbie's—they *were* Barbies. Black Barbie had brown eyes and short, textured hair that came with a pick. About her introduction to the world, A. Glenn Thomason shared her thoughts about her childhood dolls: "I had very few dolls growing up . . . a small collection of white dolls, one Barbie, and maybe one dark-colored doll. As I remember . . . everything became greatly Afrocentric and it was a big deal to see dolls of color being

> **"I am certain that simply having a black Barbie doll at a young age gave me hope that my brown skin was not the curse as viewed by society." —Sharon Raynor, professor**

Mandeville wrote in *Barbie Bazaar*, "No longer did a young black girl have to sit in the back of the bus of the American Dream." Sharon Raynor, an African American professor of English at Johnson C. Smith University remembers, "My first black Barbie blurred the lines between race, class, and gender because it became a symbol of acceptance, identity, and power. It allowed me, as a young girl, to identify with something that somewhat resembled me and to challenge the perception of others. . . . I am certain that simply having a black Barbie doll at a young age gave me hope that my brown skin was not the curse as viewed by society."

African American singer Teresa introduced on the scene. That had more of an impact on me than anything." While Black Barbie did a reasonable job reflecting at least one mainstream African American look, Hispanic Barbie pretty much missed the mark. She was dressed in a stereotypical, noncontemporary, red flouncy skirt and white peasant blouse, with a black lace shawl and red rose at the neck.

In 1982, Mattel made Magic Curl Barbie in two versions—one white and one black. The African American version of Ken also came out that year. Going forward, the company offered all of its themed dolls in both versions. A few years later, Mattel developed its line of Shani dolls, which were designed with black consumers in mind. The company hired respected African American psychologists Derek Hopson and Darlene Powell-Hopson as consultants. The Hopsons had recently re-created a study done decades earlier by African American scientists Doctors Kenneth and Mamie Clark, in which 67 percent of black children chose a white doll over a black doll, and viewed the black dolls as "ugly and bad." The Hopson study got similar results and the Hopsons were concerned about the self-esteem of these kids. Powell-Hopson said Mattel "asked us, 'What can we do that reinforces Shani in a positive way?' It shows a great deal of respect for the black community." Even the couple's young daughter helped implement change, pointing out that Mattel's commercials generally placed the black doll in the background. Mattel also had African American designer Kitty Black Perkins design clothes for the Shani line.

The three new dolls—Shani, Asha, and Nichelle—were all to have different shades of skin color, but it was even more newsworthy that Mattel planned to make these dolls a more accurate reflection of African American facial and body features. When *Newsweek* re-

Black Barbie was the first doll of color to actually be called a Barbie, as opposed to being just a friend of Barbie's.

> "Although Barbie has had friends of color since the 1960s and has herself been marketed in African American, Hispanic, and Asian versions . . . Barbie is stubbornly white. . . . No matter what racial or ethnic identity she adopts, Barbie strikes me as white-identified, as a beneficiary of white-skin privilege, as cultural evidence of white domination." —Mary F. Rogers, author of *Barbie Culture*

ported on Mattel's new dolls, the article said, "Now, ethnic Barbie lovers will be able to dream in their own image." But are people that easily classified? Professor of English and African American studies at Wesleyan University, Ann duCille writes, "Regardless of what color dyes the dolls are dipped in or what costumes they are adorned with, the image they present is of the same mythically thin, long-legged, luxuriously haired, buxom beauty." There has long been criticism that there was little difference between the original Barbie and the Barbies of color other than the amount of pigment added to a doll's mold. Upon seeing a black Astronaut Barbie at the Smithsonian, for example,

one teenage girl remarked, "Why [does Mattel] make African American Barbies with the same facial structure and hair as white Barbies, just painted black. It's such a farce. . . . black Barbies should look more like black people."

The look that Mattel came up with for the Shani dolls when they were released in 1991 may have satisfied some—Shani is a medium tone of brown. Nichelle is darker, and has a wider nose and fuller lips than the other two. Asha is light-skinned, and has the littlest nose and the thinnest lips. But when anthropologist Elizabeth Chin showed the Shani dolls to a group of African American kids in New Haven, Connecticut, one of them looked at the dolls at the toy store and assessed the situation for himself. Nichelle, he decided, was African American. But he thought Shani "must be part Indian" and Asha "is, like, Puerto Rican or a light-colored black person."

The African American kids Chin interviewed rarely had black dolls available to them, so she wondered how they played with the dolls they did have. She found that it was very common for black girls to make over their white dolls' hair with styles that better reflect their own, regardless of the skin color of the doll. These kids simply modify white dolls to suit their needs. Chin wrote, some "girls' dolls had beads in their hair, braids held at the end with twists of tin foil, and series of braids that were themselves braided together. In some sense, by doing this, the girls bring their dolls into their own worlds, and whiteness here is not absolutely defined by skin and hair, but by style and way of life."

While some girls make Barbie's hair over to match their own, others are envious of it—not necessarily the color, but the length and the texture. One teenage girl in the short film *A Girl Like Me* said, "I used to have a lot of dolls, but most of them were just white dolls with long, straight hair that I would comb, and I would be like, oh, I wish I was just like this Barbie doll." Mattel didn't dramatically change the texture of the Shani dolls' hair while they were rethinking other aspects of its face and body. Although Darlene Powell-Hopson suggested it, and they seem to have tried—Shani's hair is crimped, and comes with a hair pick—the hair is still silky. Deborah Mitchell, who is African American and was the product manager in charge of the Shani dolls said, "We added more texture. But we can't

change the fact that long, combable hair is still a key seller." And selling a product is the ultimate goal for a company. But Mattel might have made some girls happier if it had given the Shani dolls more realistic African American hair. One young girl, looking for a black Barbie doll on a toy store shelf, admitted that the reason she took her aggressions out on blonde Barbie was because of the hair. "The hair, that hair; I want it, I want it!"

One of the later Shani dolls—this line featured different shades of skin colors.

Writer Susan Jane Gilman remembered how Barbie made her feel as a kid: "We urban, Jewish, black, Asian, and Latina girls began to realize slowly and painfully that if you didn't look like Barbie, you didn't fit in. Your status was diminished. You were less beautiful, less valuable, less worthy." She continues, "I'd like to think that, two decades later, my anger about this would have cooled off—not heated up. (I mean, it's a *doll* for chrissake. Get over it.) The problem, however, is that despite all the flag-waving about multiculturalism and girls' self-esteem these days, I see a new generation of little girls receiving the same message I did twenty-five years ago."

There are collectible or special edition ethnic Barbie dolls that seem to have escaped criticism, but in part because they are so expensive, they generally don't fall under the category of toys

This Byron Lars Treasures of Africa doll is Moja, made in 2001.

for kids. Byron Lars's Treasures of Africa series includes five dolls. Mbili Barbie is very dark-skinned and has a beautiful Afro. Tatu has tight brown curls decorated with beads. Sharon Raynor owns a set of them and writes that they "represent the exquisite connection between Black American and African cultures. . . . The images of blackness are evoked in these dolls, which is refreshing to young Black girls and women."

And in 2008, Mattel made a Barbie for the one hundredth anniversary of Alpha Kappa Alpha, the first African American women's sorority. "In addition to her beauty, it is a mirror of ourselves and our beauty. It conveys a positive statement about African American girls," AKA's president Barbara McKinzie said. Sorority member Pamela Westbrooks declared, "She is beautiful in an African American woman way. . . . We think Mattel did a good job capturing the essence of an African American woman."

In 1980, Mattel began releasing its international Dolls of the World Barbies. Typically issued at least two per year, they are intended to represent various international cultures, though some of the choices seem better thought out than others. The Jamaican doll wears a traditional folk costume, although it is easy to mistake the outfit for a maid's uniform. Yla Eason, who founded Olmec Toys to make dolls of color in 1985, said, "She looks like a mammy. She's got the head rag and the apron, and I'm like, 'Why did they pick *that* slice of life?'" The descriptions on the package have sometimes encouraged stereotypes as well. In 1982, although the box that contained India Barbie said "My country has the highest mountains" and "most Indians observe the Hindu religion," it also said that most Indians "eat with their fingers" and live in houses that "don't have running water."

On the other hand, Linda Pacheco, whose husband is from Chile, was thrilled to be able to give her daughter the Chilean Barbie. She was dressed in an authentic cowgirl outfit worn at rodeos. "The huasa costume was very accurate and great for a half-Chilean girl growing up in the United States to have," Pacheco said. When Puerto Rican Barbie was introduced in 1997, Mattel consulted with the Institute of Puerto Rican Arts and Culture about the dress it chose and the text on the packaging, but there were still complaints. Interestingly, most of the people who objected to the doll were Puerto Rican women living in America. Gina

Both of these Dolls of the World sparked controversy—Jamaica (top) and Puerto Rico (bottom).

Rosario, an art director living in Virginia, said, "I was insulted. She looks very, very Anglo. . . . If you're going to represent a culture, do it properly." *New York Times* reporter Mireya Navarro had this opinion: "For many in Puerto Rico the doll is a welcome, if belated, recognition of the island's culture. But on the mainland there is a heightened sensitivity to image among Puerto Ricans who must grapple with stereotypes while trying to fit into an ethnically diverse society." The girls who live in Puerto Rico have their own opinions. Eight-year-old Amanda, who has more than forty Barbie dolls in her collection, said, "I like it more because she's from my country." Nine-year-old Krista simply said, "She has a Puerto Rican dress. She's the Puerto Rican Barbie and all the others are not."

The Dolls of the World collection was intended to celebrate global diversity. To that end, Mattel uses a variety of different face molds and skin tones. In 1981, Mattel issued the first Asian doll, meant to be from Hong Kong, which had the first Asian face mold. It had a rounder face and more almond-shaped eyes than some of the other head molds. The same face mold was then used for Japanese, Korean, and Malaysian Barbie dolls. But when real-life girls come face to face with these dolls that are meant to be "like them," it doesn't necessarily strike them that way. Fourteen-year-old Nhu shared her thoughts: "I've always hated Barbie dolls. Growing up, all I saw was the classic Barbie with her blonde hair and blue eyes. . . . But I was an Asian American, first-generation immigrant. I didn't look or live like Barbie. The more I saw this quintessential all-American girl image, the more un-

The Fulla doll, made by a Syrian company, offers Muslim children an alternative to Barbie.

The Good, the Bad, and the **BARBIE**

American I looked in my eyes. When I saw my first Asian Barbie wearing a slinky Chinese dress I certainly never wore, the feeling grew. This childhood doll supposedly manufactured to be my friend only served to make me lonelier in my new life. . . . I am American. I won't have a doll telling me 'not really.'"

At least one foreign market has created a true competitor to Barbie. In 2003, a company in Syria, NewBoy Design Studio, introduced a doll called Fulla. She was an instant hit. Fulla offered the appeal of Barbie without the affront to traditional Muslim culture that Barbie can pose. She has beautiful dark brown eyes and black hair and comes with a *hijab*—the traditional head covering worn outside the house by Islamic women—as well as a doll-size prayer mat in pink felt. Like Barbie, Fulla is sold in a pink box and has a variety of outfits to choose from, but none as revealing as what you might find on a Barbie doll. Fulla dolls—as well as backpacks, bicycles, breakfast cereals, and other Fulla merchandise—can be found all over the Middle East, Asia, and Europe. In 2007, Fulla was introduced in America.

In 2009, Mattel introduced a new

The So in Style dolls addressed some previous complaints about Mattel's dolls of color.

line of African American dolls that addressed the old complaints that some of its previous ethnic dolls looked just like blonde Barbie except for their skin tone. The So in Style dolls have fuller lips and slightly different facial structures. In addition, each of the main dolls has a distinct skin color. Two of the three have long, straight hair, but one of them, Trichelle, has curlier, more textured hair. This pleased many, but didn't go far enough for others. Black playwright Gail Parrish asked, "Why are we always pushing this standard of long hair on our girls? Why couldn't one of the dolls have a little short Afro, or shorter braids or something?" Designer Stacey McBride-Irby came up with the idea of selling the dolls in big sister/little sister pairs to promote big sisters mentoring little sisters—a value she notes as being highly regarded in the black community. The idea behind her overall design of all the dolls echoes the old phrase from the 1960s, reinforcing it for a new generation. McBride-Irby says, "I want them to see themselves within these dolls, and let them know that black is beautiful."

It's admirable that Mattel continues to work at meeting the needs of its consumers—and it makes good business sense too. But the theme of female representation in general looms even larger. There *is* no one way for a doll to represent women as a whole. It would be an insurmountable task for any company to do that. We come in too many different packages and live lives too varied for any doll to capture us—as it should be.

When Ruth and Elliot Handler started the toy company Mattel, they probably had no idea they were destined to make a doll so popular it would become a world-famous icon. This is a reproduction of the original 1959 Barbie doll.

1) These dolls are wearing vintage and reproduction outfits from the 1960s. Several of them sport the classic bubble-cut hairstyle from this era. The redhead in the middle is Barbie's best friend, Midge. 2) Registered Nurse outfit. 3) This is a vintage bubble-cut hairstyle, which was modeled after the stylish Jackie Kennedy, who was the First Lady in the early '60s. 4) These dolls are wearing some of the 1960s career outfits—there are stewardesses, a nurse, a student teacher, and even an astronaut. 5) This Barbie is wearing a reproduction of the Sleepytime Gal outfit from the '60s.

1) When Twist 'N Turn dolls first came out, girls could trade in their old Barbie for a discount on the new one. These Twist 'N Turn dolls from the 1970s include a Christie doll (right). 2) This Colored Francie doll has on a Wild Bunch outfit that captures the "Mod" feeling of the '70s. 3) Malibu Barbie came ready to hang out at the beach—already showing off her golden tan. 4) Christie was Barbie's first black friend. 5) This brunette Barbie has a hairstyle called a flip. 6) SuperStar Barbie took the '70s from Mod to Glam.

1) Flight Time Barbie and Barbie and the Rockers are great examples of the bright colors and flashy styles of the '80s.
2) and 3) NASCAR dolls roared across the finish line in 1998 and 1999. 4) One of the later Shani dolls. 5) Barbie is wearing a Stars 'n Stripes Marine Corps uniform. 6) Black Barbie was introduced in 1980 and marked the first time a Mattel doll of color was sold as an actual Barbie, not just one of her friends. 7) In the 1990s, these dolls were all about designer fashions, including clothing created by Donna Karan and Nicole Miller. Ken was the ultimate shopping accessory!

1) The three dolls in the foreground—including Ken—are Pop Life dolls that can bend every which way and do The Barbie dance. Juicy Couture Barbie and Top Model Nikki round out the group. 2–4) Close-up views of African American Christie and Redhead Kelley Pop Life dolls, as well as Top Model Nikki. 5) In 2009, Mattel launched the Barbie Basics line in a variety of skin tones. Each of the dolls comes with her own little black dress. 6) The So in Style dolls each have a little sister. They also have different hair textures and skin tones.

* Dolls of the World *

The Dolls of the World collection was first introduced in 1980 and continues to have new dolls added to it. 1) Left to right: Puerto Rican Barbie, Princess of South Africa (holding a dancing mace), Austrian Barbie, and Malaysian Barbie. 2) Malaysian Barbie. 3) Nigerian Barbie was the first black doll in this collection. 4) Back: Diwali Doll from India, Nigerian Barbie. Front: Irish Step Dancer. 5) Peruvian Barbie. 6) Polynesian Barbie. 7) Princess of South Africa.

1) Carnivale from Brazil. 2) Thai Barbie. 3) Left to right: Spanish, Polynesian, Kenyan, Thai, Canadian, Scottish, and Peruvian Barbies. 4) Back: Carnivale from Brazil Barbie, Japanese Barbie. Front: Jamaican Barbie, Native American Barbie. 5) Canadian Barbie. 6) Scottish Barbie. 7) Kenyan Barbie.

* Barbie Art *

Artist Emily Cohen's version of Mexican painter Frida Kahlo's self-portrait, entitled Barbie Becomes Frida. Cohen says, "Barbie is the ubiquitous symbol of idealized, plastic, unattainable, nonrealistic generic beauty. Frida Kahlo's image is the opposite. Kahlo's self-portraits are earthy and show her authentic beauty. When Barbie becomes Frida it is ironic because some people go to great lengths to become Barbie." Cohen made this drawing especially for The Good, the Bad, and the Barbie.

Brooklyn artist Margaux Lange's "Smiley Necklace on Torque" uses a variety of Barbie faces—from nose to chin—to create a unique and wholly original piece of wearable art. Her Plastic Body series jewelry, made entirely of Barbie parts, is showcased in art galleries and museums.

QueenSize Barb is one of 175 altered dolls in a series called The Barbs by artist Deborah Colotti. She says, "For many years, I have toyed with the Barbie icon. . . . Her life has always been stiffly perfect. Mine has not. None of my friends' lives have been either. . . . Rather than trying to make myself as frozen and superficial as a doll, I decided to make Barbie more like me."

7

Banning, Bashing, and in the Buff

FIRST OF ALL, let's just admit it: kids are always curious about anything naked. It may be a matter of seconds before a child undresses Barbie to see what's underneath those clothes. It's perfectly natural. Not that there's much to see when you strip her down to her plastic frame. Her breasts have no nipples, and most Barbies come either with underwear molded to their bodies or, as Ann duCille notes, "neither with underpants nor with a hint of anything that needs covering." Eight-year-old Liza points out, though, that she and her friends "draw on the parts, otherwise they look weird." Likewise, Ken—whom we haven't spent much time on because as fashion designer Jane Hamill said, "Barbie was never about Ken. He was always a little dusty and in the corner"—had only a slightly molded plastic bump where his private parts should be.

Nevertheless, there was no way that kids weren't going to undress them both and let their imaginations run free. And once they're undressed, it is inevitable that naked Barbie dolls will end up doing, well, naked things. In *The Barbie Chronicles*, Pamela Brandt writes, "My friends and I were not interested in Barbie's clothes. . . . We posed our naked Barbies in a variety of ways, arms twisted coyly behind their heads, legs crossed demurely at the knees, busts jutting out, innocent facsimiles of *Playboy* centerfolds." In a research study, one man recounted some of his childhood play with Barbie and Ken. His memories encompassed a wide range of activities, one

A sink full of naked Barbies is a common sight in many houses.

and Dad went around the house, then you'd let Ken and Barbie kiss." One woman recalled playing with an older boy of nine when she was about six and realizing in hindsight that their different awareness levels of sexuality were apparent. "I had the twin-size dream bed . . . and he was always . . . putting Barbie and Ken together. And I would say, 'There's only room for one.'" Author Erin Dionne also got a sneak peek at what some older kids liked to do with Barbie when she was little. "My older neighbor had a Barbie routine as stiff as the doll's joints—changing outfits, a date with Ken, then

category of which was romantic play. The researcher reported: "He often mimicked adult roles and TV shows. . . . He said that he learned the most about sex by watching soaps and mimicking what they were doing on TV."

Another woman, Janet, remembered,

"How did I . . . play with my Barbie? I took off all her clothes and sent her looking for love. My Barbie got around. . . . And it wasn't just me."
—Sarah Haskins, writer

"Of course, you wouldn't want Mom and Dad to see the things you really wanted to do with Barbie and Ken either. . . . You'd go outside and play and when Mom

the two naked and 'doing stuff' in Barbie's canopy bed. Six-year-old me found it boring and predictable—and could not understand why clacking together two nude dolls got us in trouble with her mom." Sixteen-year-old Natalie said, "My neighbor and I always had Barbie parties together because she had a ton of them, including a princess Barbie. At least, I think she was a princess, but it's hard to tell because she was always missing her clothes. We usually ended up marrying her and we were both her wives. It's kind of funny that as a child, a polygamist, nudist, homosexual lifestyle was obviously the best one, and I doubt anyone could have convinced me otherwise."

Barbie's appeal as a sex object is so ubiquitous it sneaks into our pop culture over and over again. In the sequel to *Legally Blonde*, when Elle Woods went to Washington, D.C., dressed to dazzle, one of her new coworkers sniped, "Look, it's Capitol Barbie." Journalist, comedienne, and screenwriter Sarah Haskins wrote a hilarious piece for Barbie's fiftieth birthday and addressed the issue of sex: "How did I—the daughter of a feminist and working woman, myself a future feminist and a generally liberal, Prius-driving recycling lady—play with my Barbie? I took off all her clothes and sent her looking for love. My Barbie got around. . . . And it wasn't just me. To walk into the bedroom of any of my Barbie-owning friends when I was little was to face a sordid truth. 'You want to play Barbie?' she would ask innocently and gesture. Off in the corner—a bucket of large-breasted, pants-less women."

Sometimes, just like in real life, a playmate does not appreciate romantic advances made with Barbies. Jeannette wrote to me about an incident that occurred when she was a kid: "I got my first (and only) black eye from a neighbor girl (Rosemary) when I was about nine years old. . . . I was playing 'nudist colony

Barbie and Ken share a hug before bed.

Barbie' . . . with another neighbor friend. Barbie abandoned all her fancy outfits and was vacationing in a nudist colony. My friend and I were laughing wildly and

Kids often use Barbie to role-play romantic scenarios. It's one way of imagining what adult life might be like.

having a grand silly time until Rosemary showed up and proclaimed that it was a dirty way to treat Barbie and BAM! I still think nudist colony Barbie is quite cre-ative and funny." Another creative play moment occurred when a girl named Rebecca, who always undressed her Barbie dolls, left them in a pile of naked-ness in the playroom. Her mother, Sarah, said, "Our naked Barbie collection did not go completely unnoticed. At four, my son, who was not allowed to have a toy gun, found the treasures. When he was playing with friends, he'd grab a naked Barbie, bend her at the waist, and shoot."

Being used as a toy gun is tame in comparison to some of the things kids have done to poor Barbie. In addition to romantic role-playing, mutilating Barbie dolls is another commonplace phenomenon, although sometimes what appears alarming to grown-ups has a simple explanation. A friend whose daughter was constantly popping the heads off her Barbies sat down to talk with her about it, and discovered the reason was completely benign—it is much easier to change Barbie's clothes once her head is removed, the daughter explained. When she's done dressing her, she pops it back on. The girl was also swapping Barbie heads instead of swapping outfits.

Barbie's fate often lies in the hands of boys who have been denied access to her by parents or sisters and who want to exact their revenge. She has been burned at the stake, put under the wheels of a car, torn apart, de-limbed, and flushed down the toilet. One middle-school girl said, "My brother used to torture my Barbie and I would cry." A boy of the same age reported, "When I was little, I got so mad at my little sister that I got one of her Barbies and burned her. Then my sister was calling me a murderer." Another boy added his contempt for the doll itself: "Barbie is a stupid, airhead, cheerleader

Many people think they are the only ones who tortured their dolls, but it is actually a frequent form of expression.

type of a girl. If she were real . . . she would act like all that. . . . I've pulled the heads off my sister's Barbies." Fourteen-year-old Jason wrote to me: "When I was young I had G.I. Joes and my sisters had Barbies. My army men would wage war on the Barbies (in my imagination). So whenever I got my hands on one of those shiny plastic dolls I would . . . cut it apart. When I was done I burned them so my sisters didn't know. . . . It was all a secret. They would ask where their Barbies had gone but they would find not a bit of evidence that would lead to the conclusion that I had been the mastermind behind their disappearance." Sometimes a boy is called upon to do the dirty work for a female friend. Jesse said, "I am a boy so I don't have Barbies, but my cousin did have a few so she gave me one to burn because she didn't like it. I decided to shoot it in the air with bottle rockets. When it came down it was flaming in a red glorious flame and unfortunately it was saved by a pool."

Barbie bashing seems to fall into two general categories—pure entertainment or an action that stems from something deeper. Megan had no ill will toward her dolls, yet she told me, "I'm a high-school senior but I really miss my Barbies. I loved those dolls so much, but I sure tortured them. Once I got older (like fifth or sixth grade) I reenacted the Salem witch trials with the dolls." And Chelsea shared, "When I was a kid, I liked to torture poor ol' Barbie. I know that sounds slightly like some serial-killer trait, but I assure you I'm sane. I just found it fun to cut off all of Barbie's hair and perch her on a window. Before I shoved her off." Laura, now twenty, also wrote to me: "Every little girl mutilates her toys to some ex-

tent. She pulls their stuffed tails, pokes out glass eyes, and melts plastic parts against a lightbulb. No toy, however, is more abused than a little girl's Barbie doll. I used to cut their hair. . . . My favorite pastime, however, was coloring my Barbie's hair. I used food coloring because my mother was smart enough to keep the chemicals out of my reach. My best friend came over and we attempted to give our Barbies blue streaks, pink tips, and 'all

> ## "No toy . . . is more abused than a little girl's Barbie doll."
> ### —Laura, age 20

over color' (a phrase borrowed from my mother's hairdresser). The food coloring stained my kitchen table and my mother confiscated my Barbies for a month." *Los Angeles Times* columnist Patt Morrison wrote, "She's just too unreal. How do you bond with something that looks like a taffy pull with a face? . . . Around my house, Barbie was fair game. We used her as swords, for duels. But the best was Marie Antoinette Barbie. On a scaffold built of encyclopedias, we whacked off her head but good, tiara and all, over and over again. The last couple of times, after the game got old, we got out the ketchup for a good, gory, splashy finish."

Then there are those who unleash their emotions on Barbie. Many think the brutalities Barbie suffers come from resentment toward her perfect form. Journalist Anne O'Hagan writes, "Messing with Barbie is a well-documented phenomenon and perhaps the best evidence of all that physical perfection just doesn't rate with kids." Bailey, who is in seventh grade, shared this memory: "My friend and I were at her house (I was seven) playing Barbies when we decided that we didn't like the way we looked compared to them. So we threw all of her Barbies in the toilet, ripped off all of their heads, and then threw the heads away and buried their bodies in her backyard. I think we felt intimidated by them."

Two women reflected on their Barbie bashing as kids. Dee wrote, "When I was about eight . . . I remember yanking off the limbs of my sister's Barbies and burying them in the woods around an old cabin that we had on our property. . . . I wanted nothing of the leggy, busty creature in our shared bedroom, as I knew we had nothing in common and I'd never 'blossom' into a blonde bombshell of a siren." Colleen, now grown, told me: "Let's just put it out

"Is it not a cherished part of American girlhood to dote on, dress up, play sex with, and then eventually torture Barbie with scissors and light-bulbs? Could an American girlhood be complete without this important lesson in love, accessories, and the eventual destruction—and later deconstruction—of her anatomically impossible body?"
—Sarah Goldstein, writer

there. By fourth grade I was shopping for size 10 [shoe]. Wide. I could start a car in Bedrock with my Fred Flintstones. So if there was revenge to be exacted on the pretty girl, it would be to the lower extremities. . . . I started nibbling around the ankle. My teeth sank into rubbery flesh. I thought I could explain it away as a nervous habit. But like a pen cap on test day, she was done for. I gnawed to the plastic bone of both feet, and forged a note to Ken, something about a ski accident at the chalet." And Jacklyn, who is fourteen, had mixed reasons for what she did. She told me, "The idea of dressing up Barbie in new clothes never appealed much to me or my sister. . . . [We] would come up with dangerous adventures for Barbie, which

Cutting Barbie's hair is a popular way of making Barbie into who we want her to be.

often resulted in her being burned by lava, being eaten by a T. rex, getting run over by a toy jeep, falling off a cliff, and so much more. A few times Barbie lost a leg, arm, and sometimes her head. . . . In a way we were destroying what was the impossible for any normal human being. Being blonde, perfectly tanned, and perfectly proportioned, but we mostly did it just for the enjoyment of destroying Barbie."

Lisa Jones took her anger out on the doll when, after "an 'incident' at school (where all of the girls looked like Barbie and none of them looked like me), I galloped down our stairs with one Barbie, her blonde head hitting each spoke of the banister . . . until her head popped off, lost to the graveyard behind the stairwell. Then I tore off each limb, and sat on the stairs for a long time twirling the torso like a baton." Santha Cassell, a high-school English teacher, offered this memory: "I asked for Barbie dolls, but then mutilated the ones my mother grudgingly bought for me—until she stopped buying them. I believe by mutilating them I might have been in solidarity with my mother. I never fit in. I didn't know how other girls played with them. They were just so bashable, and although I wasn't aware of it at the time, I was probably angry because of the doll's looks."

**"They were just so bashable."
—Santha Cassell, teacher**

Two studies looked at this topic, with interesting results. One, conducted at the University of Bath by Dr. Agnes Nairn, was actually accidental. Nairn and her colleagues were researching which products seven- to eleven-year-old children thought were "cool" or "not cool." Amid images of many items, there were pictures of Barbie. The reactions to these pictures astonished them. Nairn said, "The doll provoked rejection, hatred, and violence." Many girls reported torturing Barbie and the most-cited reason in Nairn's study had nothing to do with body image or feelings of inadequacy. Instead, Nairn said, "The most readily expressed reason for rejecting Barbie was that she was babyish." They had grown out of Barbie and she had therefore become expendable. In another study, researchers also found that most of the torture play was done by girls who used to play with Barbie but no longer had much use for her. In addition, when the girls felt angry or hurt in general—even though the feelings may not have been caused by or directed at Barbie—they took their aggressions out on the doll.

Adults do some Barbie bashing of their own, and anger or frustration generally *is* the root cause when they take action. Patt Morrison is in favor of having "a go at Barbie." In 2006, after Mattel announced another Barbie makeover, she responded in her newspaper column: "Send her to her death. Stage a state funeral worthy of the super-toy she is. Give her a lethal injection, put Barbie on the barbie, put out a hit on her—just do it." In 2009, one adult's distaste for the doll went so far as to prompt him to suggest banning Barbie altogether. U.S. representative Jeff Eldridge, from West Virginia, knew he would be criticized, but felt strongly enough about gathering support and making his opinion public that he formally proposed a Barbie Ban Bill. He said, "I knew a lot of people were going to joke about it and poke fun at me. I couldn't get anybody to sign on the bill with me, but I said I'm still going to introduce it." And he did. Although it didn't go any further, Eldridge sent the Barbie Ban Bill to the House Judiciary Committee in March 2009.

Everyone suffers from insecurities, and it can be helpful for kids to express their frustrations about the expectations that society places upon them. Barbie is a willing scapegoat. She is malleable and her smile stays intact no matter what. And sometimes, perhaps, we make too much out of analyzing what it all means. Kids are well aware that Barbie is not real, that they are not taking their aggressions out on anything that can actually feel the effects. Columnist Ann Treneman reminds us, "Have we all forgotten what it is like to play with dolls? . . . My sisters and I treated our dolls appallingly. We had tea parties, yes, but we also had a theatre of war. Dolls were routinely kidnapped and attacked. Several were scalped and at least one was mutilated beyond repair. It was hardly pretty or nice."

8

Barbie as Art

BEING THE POPULAR, perfect girl makes Barbie easy to hate. She also serves as a creative outlet for many different types of artists. She inspires writers as well as visual and performing artists, showing up in books, movies, and museums. Barbie has become a medium with which to make a point. Steven Dubin, a sociology professor at Columbia, described why artists have been so enthralled with Barbie over the years: "Anytime you've got something which seems to solidify what an ideal form is supposed to be—you had Venus de Milo in the past, now you've got Barbie—it's the perfect thing for artists to play with . . . it's a gift to artists, in fact."

In literature, she appears in several works, such as *Mondo Barbie: An Anthology of Fiction and Poetry* and *The Barbie Chronicles*, a collection of essays from different authors. In many instances, writers who played with Barbie while growing up attribute their skills and desire to write, in part, to their early times with the doll. Megan McCafferty, best-selling author of *Sloppy Firsts* and the rest of the Jessica Darling series, said, "For as much as I've heard Barbies maligned as antifeminist playthings, I know my dolls provided a positive conduit for the development of my youthful storytelling skills."

Laurie Faria Stolarz, author of books for teens such as the *Blue Is for Nightmares* series and *Project 17*, sent a love letter of sorts to Barbie, thanking her for acting as her muse. "Dear Barbie, I can hardly believe that I've never even dedicated a single title to you—you, who helped make me a writer; who played with me for hours on end; and who starred in my every dramatic performance. . . . I don't know where I'd be if I hadn't had you in my life. . . . I owe you a lot—probably more than you'll ever know. Love always, Laurie Faria Stolarz." The author who

feeling that they painted Barbie in a bad light, and sued the group. Aqua, in turn, sued Mattel. The lawsuits were thrown out, and in language rarely, if ever, heard in court the judge scolded, "The parties are advised to chill." In keeping with the "love to hate" phenomenon that often surrounds Barbie, the song went on to make *Rolling Stone*'s 20 Most Annoying Songs list of 2007, was chosen as one of

> "I'm convinced I became a novelist by playing with Barbie and constructing elaborate narratives around her."
> —Yona Zeldis McDonough, author of *The Barbie Chronicles*

compiled *The Barbie Chronicles*, Yona Zeldis McDonough, has similar sentiments. On the occasion of Barbie's fiftieth birthday, she said, "I'm convinced I became a novelist by playing with Barbie and constructing elaborate narratives around her." If she could send a birthday wish, says McDonough, "It would be, you go, girl. And you keep on going."

Barbie is a hit in the performing arts world too. She was the muse for the Danish pop group Aqua. Their song "Barbie Girl" was released in 1997 and climbed the charts all over the world. Mattel didn't appreciate the lyrics, though,

Blender magazine's 50 Worst Songs Ever in 2009, and sold more than eight million copies.

The song was so catchy, in fact, that Mattel came around in 2009 and officially adapted it for a marketing campaign for a new line of Barbie doll with twelve points of movement so kids can make it dance. "The beauty of Barbie," Mattel spokesperson Stephanie Cota said about the song dispute, is that she can "kiss and make up." Mattel used the new version of the song for a music video that appeared first on YouTube, then in television commercials. Some of the lyrics were changed to continue Barbie's long-term motto that girls "can do anything." But perhaps the most memorable line from the original lyrics remained intact: "Life in plastic, it's fantastic." In the video, Barbie dolls and real women do "The Barbie" to the beat. Mattel cleverly hired rising choreographer star JaQuel Knight—who shot to fame after choreographing Beyoncé's hit "Single Ladies (Put a Ring on It)"— to create The Barbie. There is even an instructional video on YouTube in which Knight breaks down the dance so everyone can learn how to do it.

Performance artists are forever making Barbie their own, from drag queens in clubs to street performers. They each have their own statement to make about the doll. Filmmakers have also used the doll as a jumping-off point. One movie, called *The Tribe*, which lasts only eighteen minutes, was written by Ken Goldberg and Tiffany Shlain—a husband-and-wife team. Shlain was fascinated by what she considered "one of the greatest ironies of pop culture: that the creator of Barbie was Jewish." Ironic because Barbie, especially in the blonde form, looks more like a German beauty ideal than any image found in Jewish history.

A still from the 2006 movie The Tribe, which explored the connection between Barbie and being Jewish in America.

Shlain said, "It hit me that Barbie, the ultimate assimilated Jew, was the perfect tool to explore these issues of assimilation." The 2006 film won many prestigious awards and its creators say they made it to spark discussion about what it means to be Jewish in America today.

Another film that triggered both conversation and controversy when it came out in 1987 was *Superstar: The Karen Carpenter Story*. Todd Haynes created this disturbing yet sensitive documentary about the singer and her battle with anorexia. He used a combination of live footage and animated scenes with Barbie dolls and dioramas to create the simple, spare, yet powerful film. In one frame, a block of text interrupts the action and describes how the pressure to have the "perfect" body can be even harder on a celebrity constantly in the spotlight than it is for other girls. Haynes shows the Carpenter doll becoming upset after a reporter calls her "chubby," and this seems to mark the beginning of her struggle with the illness. Karen Carpenter's brother, Richard, the other half of their musical group, was so distressed by the film that he took

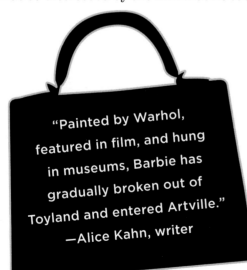

"Painted by Warhol, featured in film, and hung in museums, Barbie has gradually broken out of Toyland and entered Artville."
—Alice Kahn, writer

legal action and Haynes stopped showing the movie.

There is an abundance of visual art that uses Barbie's image too. In San Francisco, there is an annual Altered Barbie Exhibition, which includes music, films, and performance art, as well as paintings and sculpture. Curator Julie Andersen said, "The concept of altering Barbie, of turning her into a piece of art, brings it into the realm of personal identity." Some of the pieces are fashion statements, while others take a different approach. "I spend my time trying to alter the Barbie image by making Barbie into a warrior . . . fattening her, giving her more muscle," one of the artists, Debbie Fimrite, said. She adds, "Sometimes I try to make her more like the actual people in my life because I am so sick of the blonde princess image and the glamour queen doll I grew up with." Melissa Chow took a series of photographs of Barbie and said, Barbie "represents the good and the bad stereotypes of culture, race, materialism, womanhood. In that sense, I find something amusing and gratifying about altering something so solidly representative of old-fashioned values."

Craig Yoe, author of *The Art of Barbie*, said, "Barbie has to be the perfect photographer's model. She never has an extra pound or an unsightly pimple, and she can hold a pose perfectly still." He is one of many men who were told not to play with Barbie when they were young. In the foreword of his book, Yoe wrote, "I was always forced to admire Her from afar. . . . So . . . I know I wasn't supposed to Play Barbie . . . but, it was every bit as exciting and fun as I had imagined. Sorry, Mom." Another photographer, Tom Forsythe, took a series of images called "Food Chain Barbie" that bothered Mattel. It included such

Left: Artist Deborah Colotti's QueenSize Barb. Above: "Colossus of Barbie" is a sculpture made from plaster, sand, and wood, by Robert Stern.

"No matter what I did, it kept smiling." —Tom Forsythe, artist

photos as "Heatwave," which had her roasting in a rotisserie oven. Forsythe said, "I put the doll in situations that would be jarring, and ways that didn't fit the image that Mattel was trying to create for the doll, because I felt that was a false image." The artist came up with his idea, in part, when it irked him that no matter the abuse Barbie takes, she keeps on smiling. He said, "There was the stupid smile. No matter what I did, it kept smiling. Of course, it is not real. It is not a person; it is only a bit of plastic. I wanted to tell people that Barbie is just an advertising vehicle, not something to emulate."

Some of the three-dimensional art inspired by Barbie includes a version of

Left: Margaux Lange in her studio, surrounded by her Barbie bins.
Above: Lange's Busted Heart necklace.

the ancient Greek statue of the Venus de Milo by Dean Brown and a series of figures called "The Barbs," by artist Deborah Colotti, which are her imaginings of "Barb in the real world." She said, "Rather than trying to make myself as frozen and superficial as a doll, I decided to make Barbie more like me. And more like the lives I see around me every day." Some of her interpretations are violent or disturbing, but others take on more common issues. The artist explained, "She has acne, gets fat, and becomes old and wrinkled."

There is even wearable art with a Barbie theme. Margaux Lange has been playing with Barbie since she was a little girl—but her collection is much bigger now. The thirty-year-old has a full-time career as an artist and jewelry designer, making earrings, bracelets, and necklaces out of Barbie parts. She gets her dolls from a multitude of sources—people give them to her and she scoops them up whenever she can at yard sales and online. As the dolls come in, she strips them of their clothes and accessories and separates their heads from their bodies so the heads don't get crushed in her bins full of bodies. When she is ready to sort them more specifically, the various parts go into plastic bins with labels such as BUSTS AND BUTTS, EYE IN PAIRS, and MOUTHS WITH TEETH. It is not surprising that Barbie showed up in Lange's artwork in high school and while she studied at the Maryland Institute College of Art, as she admits to "a childhood spent obsessed with Barbie and her miniature world." Her pursuit helped her explore a "love-hate relationship: fond childhood memories balanced against adult discomfort with the doll as a problematic role model." Today, her Plastic Body Series jewelry has been featured in books and magazines, and shown at art galleries and museums.

This self-described feminist was taken aback, though, when chatter on a feminist blog criticized her work as being objectionable to women. Some people saw her jewelry, which is made out of Barbie eyes, smiles, legs, arms, hands, and other parts, as reducing women to a series of body parts. Others disagreed, saying that they saw Lange's work as feminist and that she was using pieces of a doll, not a woman. I asked Lange to explain her point of view, and she said, "I don't believe it's fair to say that *all* partial representations of women's bodies are necessarily an objectification of women, especially when considered in an artistic context." She added, "Some people have

"MY OBSESSION WITH Barbie as a kid had been this incredibly positive, fulfilling, creative experience, and yet now in adulthood, I started to wonder . . . had Barbie actually messed me up somehow? Was she more problematic than I was recognizing? Despite self-identifying as a feminist since the age of fifteen, I questioned what my relationship to the doll meant to me and to my understanding of feminism. I wondered what (if any) role she played in regards to my self-esteem and my sense of what it meant to be a 'Woman.' Could I still be a feminist if I was also a fan of Barbie? My jewelry collection spawned from all that questioning."

—Margaux Lange, jewelry designer

a hard time separating Barbie from a real woman, which only further indicates the amount of humanness we have attached to this inanimate object. I find this fascinating."

A few artists place Barbie in well-known images of art, such as Emily Cohen in *Birth of Barbie*, in which the artist renders Barbie standing in a half-shell on the shore of the ocean, where the goddess Venus stands in Sandro Botticelli's *The Birth of Venus*. (Cohen was inspired to create a new image upon learning about this book. See page 82 for her *Barbie Becomes Frida*.) Barbie has even captivated the ultrafamous American pop artists Peter Max and Andy Warhol. Max painted Barbie in 1994 and said, "The show with [Barbie's] paintings became one of the most attended shows of all." Mattel CEO Jill Barad commissioned Warhol to paint Barbie's portrait. It hung in Barad's office for several years and was showcased in March 2009, when it graced Jonathan Adler's life-size Dream House in Malibu for Barbie's fiftieth birthday party. All of these works of art indicate Barbie's iconic status and show how connected to our culture the doll is, and is likely to remain.

Artist Andy Warhol displays his portrait of Barbie in 1986.

9

A Real Doll

THERE ARE LITERALLY thousands of newspaper and magazine articles, as well as academic papers and books that put Barbie at the center of discussion. Why does she irritate—even enrage—so many people and attract so many others to leap to her defense? She is just a doll, after all. But she is *not* just a doll. Yes, Mattel made her an icon, but not without help. It started at the moment of her inception. That very first television commercial, with Barbie as an active companion, planted the illusion in our minds that she was "real." The idea was so powerful, it stuck.

Mattel reinforced the desire in us to make Barbie real by creating an entire life story for her. A series of novels published in the 1960s established who she was, complete with a birth date, parents, and a significant other—Ken. According to the novels, Barbara (aka Barbie) Millicent Roberts grew up in Willows, Wisconsin, where she lived with her parents George and Margaret Roberts. She later attended Manhattan International High School, which was based on Stuyvesant High School in New York City. The novels establish Barbie as a modern, independent kind of girl who was not going to be bound by the 1950s stereotypes she felt kept her mother tied to the house. In *Barbie's New York Summer*, she goes from Wisconsin to New York City to work as a model. During a heart-to-heart talk, Barbie asks her mother whether she ever had dreams of her

own, and her mother replied, "I have you till you're grown and I have Dad. You're the one who has an exciting career ahead of you." Today, there are new books and movies starring Barbie, and she's online, too. We have bought into the idea of Barbie being a "real" doll and helped make her the icon—and subject of controversy—that she is.

Barbie isn't the only one with a story. Others were frequently introduced to her circle of family and friends—building on the illusion that Barbie was real—and they all came with an explanation as to how they fit in. When Mattel presented a new doll in Barbie's life, there was a brief script that went along with it, usually on the back of the box. Ken was introduced first, in 1962, after consumers clamored for Barbie to have a boyfriend. But everyone knows a girl needs a best friend even more than a boyfriend, so in 1963, Midge came along, in part to combat criticism that Barbie was too sexy. Midge's face was fuller than Barbie's, and usually dotted with freckles, but she had the same proportions as Barbie so they could share clothes. All that fuss over the Barbie body, and it turns out the only differences in Midge were from the neck up.

A year after Midge, Barbie got a little sis-

Top: Barbie wears a reproduction of a 1960s "Open Road" outfit.
Bottom: Fans wanted Barbie to have a boyfriend, so Ken came on the scene in 1962.

ter, Skipper. Since Skipper was only nine inches tall, Barbie's clothes didn't fit her, but they did coordinate with little sis's wardrobe. And pretty soon, there were more kids in the family. The twins Tutti and Todd were Barbie's brother and sister. They were "born" in 1966 and measured only six inches tall. Just like their big sister did, Skipper, Tutti, and Todd had their share of pals such as Skipper's boyfriend, Ricky, and her best friend, Skooter. And the list went on. Sometimes it was hard to keep up with all of Barbie's family and friends. Ann Treneman wrote, "Never has a doll had her family extended so ruthlessly. Every year the company creates yet more cousins and siblings for Barbie, not to mention outfits, pets, nationalities, and careers. If Barbie were real she would have a nervous breakdown about it all, renounce pink for life, and tell her ineffectual boyfriend Ken that it's all over."

Left: Best friend Midge had the same body as Barbie, but no one seemed to mind. Above: Skipper, Stacie, and Todd were some of Barbie's siblings.

✳ ✳ ✳

In the history of all that is Barbie, the doll and her gang weren't the only ones with dramas playing out. As brilliant as Mattel was at making and marketing toys, there was trouble lurking behind what seemed to be a Cinderella story. By 1970, Ruth Handler had become president of the company with more than a dozen vice presidents in her charge, and the Handlers had branched out into all kinds of interesting ventures such as helping to produce the kids' movie

> "She is hardly going to fade away. . . . But she is not real, and another thing that must be faced is that little girls know this. . . . Little girls take something that is unreal, like Barbie, and make her real through play and neglect. . . . All we are talking about here is a bit of curved plastic who has managed to achieve icon status by decades of clever marketing."
> —Ann Treneman, writer

Sounder, acquiring a handful of European toy companies, and creating multiple divisions within their ever-growing company. But many of the companies Mattel bought did not do well, a fire ruined one of its factories along with all the toys inside, and the number of sales predicted began to be higher than the number of orders received. To make Mattel look more profitable than it was, someone in the financial department falsified records.

And then it all began to catch up to them. In March 1972, Mattel announced a major loss for the first time ever. The price of Mattel's stock began to go down. The following year, after Elliot announced things were improving, he had to take it back, and Mattel issued another statement saying it had suffered another loss. Ruth remembered, "All hell broke loose. . . . We were out of control and did not really know how badly."

Lawsuits were filed, and Mattel came under investigation for fraud. As president, Ruth was in the hot seat. But she was adamant that all she had done was follow the advice of her financial advisors. Although Ruth was probably not the person who initiated the illegal accounting methods that had gotten Mattel in trouble, it was unlikely that she hadn't known anything about them. Still, she issued a press release declaring her innocence—a stand she never backed down from. But as the president of the company at the time when the financial problems were occurring, Ruth was held accountable. Within the company, people either avoided her or ignored her. "It was a very demeaning, humiliating experience," she said. And in 1975, she and Elliot resigned from Mattel. "It was heartbreaking. By the time we left I was devastated," Ruth said. Four years later, she was convicted of fraud, charged a fine, and ordered to do five hundred hours of community service each year, for five years. In other words, she was found guilty. "She always denied it, and I don't think she instigated the fraud," Robin Gerber, author of *Barbie and Ruth,* wrote. But, she added, "There's no way a woman who knew where every company penny was going could miss the fact that millions of dollars of claimed sales didn't really exist."

For several years, Ruth had been fighting breast cancer. On June 16, 1970, her left breast was removed. At that time, mastectomies were sometimes kept secret and women often felt ashamed and disfigured. Ruth was scared and depressed. She went back to work in late July of that year, but later wrote, "I was unable to speak with authority. I lost the courage of my convictions." Ruth, who had always been so strong and proud, felt defeated.

True to form, though, after battling breast cancer, going through the difficulties with Mattel, and defending herself, she bounced back. Just one day after leaving Mattel, in fact, she met with the man who had made her prosthetic (artificial) breast, and announced, "I'm going into the breast business." Ruth disliked the unnatural and uncomfortable feeling of the prostheses available to women who

Top: Ruth Handler models one of the Nearly Me prosthetic bras she designed for women with mastectomies. Bottom: In 1999, Ruth joined in the fortieth-anniversary celebration of Barbie.

had mastectomies and decided right on the spot that she was going to design one that would make a woman feel beautiful again. She called her company Ruthton, since "Ruth" had not been worked into the Mattel name, and named her product Nearly Me. Ruth had found a new mission, and a new insight into herself.

Along the way, this smart, tough woman, who was not used to forming close ties with other women, began to figure out how important they were to her. About Nearly Me fittings, Ruth said, "To take a woman who comes in . . . often she will be quite hostile or confused or uptight or all so unsure of herself. I take that woman . . . through a fitting, have a happy experience where at the end she's laughing and joking and sticking her chest out and showing off what she's wearing. . . . She gives me that look and a hug and a kiss. I never see her again [but] that's my high."

In the 1990s, hard feelings in the past, Ruth was welcomed back into the Mattel fold and celebrated as the mother of Barbie. She was featured at conventions and signed countless autographs. Ruth also began to repair her long-strained relationship with her daughter, Barbara. "Both of us decided," Barbara said, "that we weren't going to get at each other anymore." Ruth had reinvented herself and found her way back, living out new dreams and enjoying her family, which now included grandchildren. In April 2002, this unique and unabashed fighter passed away. Later that year, when Barbie had her tiny plastic hand- and footprints cemented for all time in Hollywood, Ruth's daughter, Barbara, was there to honor her mother.

As for Barbie, screenwriter Robin

Swicord said, "Barbie is bigger than all those executives. She has lasted through many regimes. She's lasted through neglect. . . . She's survived the feminist backlash. Barbie embodies not a cultural view of femininity but the essence of woman." Barbie will probably never stop reinventing herself. After all, a girl has to keep up with the changing times.

So is Barbie positive, negative . . . or both? It all depends on the point of view. But girls figure out who they want to be by trying things on for size, acting things out. By seeing how it feels to put

In 2002, Barbara Handler appeared on behalf of her late mother to dip Barbie's hands and feet in cement on Hollywood Boulevard.

on makeup, being a girly girl, being a tomboy, pretending to be a flight attendant, a race car driver, an astronaut, a housewife. Playing with Barbie lets them experiment with all things feminine. They impose their will upon Barbie—not the other way around. Girls are strong, and no plastic, eleven-and-a-half-inch doll could ever change that.

Part of the 2010 Barbie Basic line.

A Note from the Author

THROUGHOUT THE RESEARCH and writing of this book, I was repeatedly asked how an author who writes about strong women got it in her head to do a book about Barbie. Or, as one person put it, "How are you going to write anything positive?" When I laughed, he added, "No, really, I'm not kidding. What's good about Barbie?"

First, as we have seen, Ruth Handler was indeed a strong, independent, determined woman who built one of the biggest toy companies in the world through sheer intention to succeed, savvy business sense, and relentless hard work. Second, the initial idea for this book came when I suggested to my editor, Catherine Frank, that Barbie be my next subject in the "Up Close" series, for which I had recently written *Ella Fitzgerald*. Catherine began to laugh before realizing that I was not, in fact, kidding. "Come on," I said, "consider the criteria for the series. An American icon, which kids and teens are familiar with and that has made a significant impact on our culture. That says Barbie to me, all the way." Because Catherine is wise and open-minded, laughter quickly turned to discussion. In the end, we agreed that Barbie would seem out of place among the other "Up Close" figures such as John F. Kennedy and Thurgood Marshall, but became excited about pursuing the topic as a stand-alone title. And that's where the fun began.

Little did I know the chord I would strike by putting out the word that I was working on a Barbie book. People started forwarding me news stories, cartoons, hilarious images—everyone wanted to share. Everyone wanted to *play*. And in so many different ways! Within two weeks, more than three hundred anecdotes from students, teachers, librarians, and writers flooded my inbox. And they just kept coming. Their voices were clamoring to be heard. All I had to do was say "Barbie" and people would launch into their stories. As they poured in, it was eye-opening to discover how passionate people are—they either Love Her or Hate Her. There is not much middle-of-the-road when it comes to Barbie. This realization reminded me of something my dad told me during my impressionable twenties, when I was upset by someone's (obviously misguided) opinion of me—that however many people there were out in the world who knew me, there would be that many different perspectives of who I am. We all impose our own ideas and perceptions on the world, and Barbie may just be the ultimate scapegoat.

My own experiences with Barbie were not particularly dramatic, although the fact that I chose not to play with her when my sister had plenty of Barbies around may say something. I don't recall having strong feelings about her one way or the other, but I felt this made me a good candidate to be objective and look at all sides of the issues I was interested in exploring, such as body image, role-playing, and ethnicity. Within these pages, you heard from boys, girls, men, and women about the impact Barbie has had on *them*. Opinions were just about split down the middle between positive and negative. But one thing was clear to me: Barbie is an American icon, and it is worth examining why she inspires such distress—and such devotion.

$\mathcal{A}$CKNOWLEDGMENTS

✻

THERE ARE TWO features of this book that have made this experience more wholly unique and thoroughly interesting than I could ever have imagined. One is the original quoted material from the many people who had such strong feelings about Barbie—both pro and con—that they were moved to share their memories and anecdotes with me. I thank you all for your willingness to add your thoughts to the discussion, which enhanced it in a remarkable and personal way.

The second is the abundance of new photos we were able to create of the doll, thanks to the photographic artistry of Karen Pike Photography and the generous spirit and playful nature of Peter Harrigan, theater professor at Saint Michael's College, in Vermont, and the proud owner of the Barbie collection featured in this book. Peter, I thank you for sharing your knowledge and expertise, as well as all the time you spent with me as we chose the dolls to include from your collection, readied them for their close-ups, and put together a fabulous photo shoot!

I would also like to thank Emily Colleen McWilliams for her research assistance at the Schlesinger Library at Harvard University.

Source Notes

*

A NOTE ABOUT the sources: Many of the personal quotes are a result of direct e-mail correspondence between the author and people who wanted to weigh in on the topics being discussed. As many of the quotes were sent by students, and in order to protect people's privacy, we have often included only first names and ages in the text, and have refrained from documenting private e-mail addresses in these source notes.

ENDPAPERS

"We made her quite bland . . .": Stern, *Barbie Nation*.

"I never had a problem . . .": E-mail to author.

"I expect that several thousand . . .": E-mail to author.

"Barbie gave us no messages . . .": Lefkof, "Barbie (and Ken) Raised My Consciousness."

"Kids don't nurture . . ." O'Hagan, "Toying with Perfection."

"Barbie has been the #1 most . . .": E-mail to author.

"If Barbie is a monster . . .": duCille, "Dyes and Dolls."

"Barbie . . . seemed to demand . . .": Rand, *Barbie's Queer Accessories*, 98.

"Society *made* Barbie . . .": BillyBoy, *Barbie: Her Life and Times*, 44.

"Girls learn how to be women . . .": McDonough, *The Barbie Chronicles*, 113.

"I hate Barbie . . .": Quindlen, "Public & Private."

"Her teeth were . . .": E-mail to author.

"Barbie is really only a reflection . . .": E-mail to author.

"Her shape is as recognizable . . .": Morrison, "Barbie Must Die."

"Barbie, I hate you!" E-mail to author.

PROLOGUE

"Barbie really means . . .": Champion Media radio broadcast, 5/17/09.

"Barbie has been the #1 most . . .": E-mail to author.

"I could search the whole world . . .": E-mail to author.

"When I was younger . . .": E-mail to author.

"My sister and I . . ." and "I never once admired . . .": "Barbie Turns 50," NPR Radio.

"I think Barbie really . . .": Kauffman, "Birthday Girl Barbie."

"Barbie has always . . .": Handler, *Dream Doll*, 43.

CHAPTER 1

"It has been suggested . . .": Handler, *Dream Doll*, 15.

"I guess I've had this . . .": Gerber, *Barbie and Ruth*, 25.

"the greatest influence . . .": Handler, *Dream Doll*, 16.

"Sarah was just trying . . .": Gerber, *Barbie and Ruth*, 25.

"[Sarah] was a fantastic . . .": and "To me, they seemed . . .": Handler, *Dream Doll*, 16.

"treated like a . . .": Gerber, *Barbie and Ruth*, 25.

"I used to love it. . . .": Gerber, *Barbie and Ruth*, 26.

"simply preferred working . . ." and "It's not that I . . .": Handler, *Dream Doll*, 17.

"I didn't like dolls . . .": Handler, *Dream Doll*, 17–18.

"My father loved to . . .": Handler, *Dream Doll*, 18–19.

"I loved every minute . . .": Handler, *Dream Doll*, 19.

"They liked him as . . .": Handler, *Dream Doll*, 22.

"Cross your fingers . . .": Handler, *Dream Doll*, 25.

"Though I really hadn't . . .": Handler, *Dream Doll*, 28.

"While out for my first . . .": Handler, *Dream Doll*, 20.

CHAPTER 2

"He was poor and . . .": Stern, *Barbie Nation*.

"I was fit to be tied . . .": Gerber, *Barbie and Ruth*, 55.

"Though I dearly loved . . .": Handler, *Dream Doll*, 44.

"missed the fast-paced . . .": Handler, *Dream Doll*, 47.

"I was frightened . . .": Gerber, *Barbie and Ruth*, 63.

"Oh, how I hated . . .": Gerber, *Barbie and Ruth*, 80.

"When it came to being . . . ": Gerber, *Barbie and Ruth*, 67.

"He was, unquestionably, . . .": Gerber, *Barbie and Ruth*, 82.

"Yes, it was Elliot's . . .": Gerber, *Barbie and Ruth*, 59.

"We knew every single . . .": Gerber, *Barbie and Ruth*, 89.

"It's not that we . . ." and "It was unheard of . . .": Handler, *Dream Doll*, 76.

"A tour of your plant . . .": Gerber, *Barbie and Ruth*, 86.

"I know that my life . . .": Handler, *Dream Doll*, 76.

"I don't think you . . ." and "It was the easiest . . .": Gerber, *Barbie and Ruth*, 97.

"By the day before . . .": Handler, *Dream Doll*, 84.

"Things got pretty bleak . . .": Gerber, *Barbie and Ruth*, 98.

"It was like the roof . . .": Gerber, *Barbie and Ruth*, 99.

CHAPTER 3

"those who longed for . . .": Koss, "My Barbie."

"Do you really want to . . .": Loughrey, "Hello Dolly."

"[Barbara and her friends] would sit . . .": Lord, *Forever Barbie*, 30.

"Ruth, no mother is . . .": Gerber, *Barbie and Ruth*, 7–8.

"We haven't superimposed . . .": Lord, *Forever Barbie*, 42.

"My daughter would be . . .": Lord, *Forever Barbie*, 39.

"It has too much of a . . ." and "I don't like the influence . . .": Miller, *Toy Wars*, 69.

"snobbish" and "sharp": Lord, *Forever Barbie*, 30.

"Ruth lit one cigarette . . .": Gerber, *Barbie and Ruth*, 2.

"For the most part . . .": Gerber, *Barbie and Ruth*, 18.

"She was very . . .": Gerber, *Barbie and Ruth*, 19.

"To first-generation Barbie owners . . .": Lord, *Forever Barbie*, 9.

"When school was out . . .": Lord, *Forever Barbie*, 43.

"I was the first girl . . .": E-mail to author.

"My Barbie was an early . . .": E-mail to author.

"As a kid I loved my . . .": E-mail to author.

CHAPTER 4

"I just wanted . . ." "I don't take fashion . . ." and "I dressed them . . .": Loughrey, "Hello Dolly."

"The new spring clothes . . ." and "When you're a young girl . . .": BillyBoy, *Barbie: Her Life and Times*, 22.

"Barbie was her own . . .": Lord, *Forever Barbie*, 9.

"Those original Charlotte Johnson . . .": Westenhouser, *The Story of Barbie*, 160.

"Sure, her changing . . .": Phelan, "Feminists and Fan Both Ask: 'Will the Real Barbie Step Forward?'"

"You get hooked on . . .": Gerber, *Barbie and Ruth*, 150.

"My grandmother made . . .": Vander Broek and Noer, "Barbie Turns 50."

"Thinking of Barbie . . .": Rogers, *Barbie Culture*, 28.

"I still have . . .": E-mail to author.

"My mother made . . .": E-mail to author.

"Barbie is where your . . .": Vander Broek and Noer, "Barbie Turns 50."

"I had a friend . . .": Rand, *Barbie's Queer Accessories*, 96.

"I didn't want to take . . .": Rand, *Barbie's Queer Accessories*, 97.

"Barbies are a total waste . . .": E-mail to author.

"Although Barbie has . . .": Jones and Newman, "Hello, Dolly!"

"I really love that . . .": Brett, "Barbie's the Birthday Doll."

"This is an inspiration . . ." "Why is beauty . . ." "Real astronauts do not . . ." "I fail to see . . ." "Oh, gee—Flight . . ." "Appreciate the gender-flipping . . .": Pekarik, "Understanding Visitor Comments."

"To my baby boomer mom . . .": Haskins, "Barbie's Little Secret."

CHAPTER 5

"are all perfect . . ." and "She is like the . . .": Kuther and McDonald, "Early Adolescents' Experiences with, and Views of, Barbie."

"Barbie was never a . . .": E-mail to author.

"Barbie was who I . . .": E-mail to author.

"When I was little . . .": E-mail to author.

"may never find relief . . .": Rogers, *Barbie Culture*, 118

"Women's dislike of their . . .": Rogers, *Barbie Culture*, 133

"Unlike our foremothers . . ." and "The sum total . . .": Martin, *Perfect Girls, Starving Daughters*, 147.

"look as good as . . .": *The Insider*, "Heidi Klum Zeroed by Size Zero."

"We didn't fully consider . . .": "Mattel Says It Erred," *New York Times*.

"Today's media floods us . . .": Jones and Newman, "Hello, Dolly!"

"perpetuated sexual stereotypes . . .": "Feminists Protest 'Sexist' Toys in Fair," *New York Times*.

"Barbie-free . . ." "I hate Barbie . . ." and "To get rid of Barbie . . .": Quindlen, "Public & Private; Barbie at 35."

"As one who consumed . . .": Lefkof, "Barbie (and Ken) Raised My Consciousness."

"Oh, Mama, don't be . . .": Quindlen, "Public & Private; Barbie at 35."

"With her nonfunctional body . . .": Treneman, "Time to Stop Hating Barbie."

"a raging . . ." "being obsessed" and "She was beautiful . . .": Loughrey, "Hello Dolly."

"If she [a girl] was going to . . .": Kershaw, "Ruth Handler, Whose Barbie Gave Dolls Curve, Dies at 85."

"I wanted little girls who . . ." and "With each passing year, . . .": Stern, "*Barbie Nation*."

"My relationship with Barbie . . .": Brett, "Barbie's the Birthday Doll."

"Some grown-ups say . . .": "Through Her 50 Years on Toy-Store Shelves . . . ," *National Review.*

"akin to those . . ." and "Through Barbie I . . .": E-mail to author.

"When I was a kid, . . .": E-mail to author.

"I never felt . . .": E-mail to author.

"Barbie's body never made . . .": E-mail to author.

"I wasn't bothered . . .": E-mail to author.

"I remember distinctly . . .": E-mail to author.

"I'd rather have my . . .": E-mail to author.

"I'm sure my mother . . .": E-mail to author.

"rarely talked, making . . ." "to see what it . . ." and "turning herself into . . .": Chamberlain, "Idollatry."

"We came to the idea . . .": Martin, *Perfect Girls, Starving Daughters*, 74.

"My mommy says men . . ." and "And they blame . . .": Lord, *Forever Barbie*, 84.

"I would love to say . . .": E-mail to author.

"Barbie has this perfect . . .": Kuther and McDonald, "Early Adolescents' Experiences with, and Views of, Barbie."

"You never see a fat . . .": Chin, "Ethnically Correct Dolls: Toying with the Race Industry."

"Barbie comes in only . . .": E-mail to author.

"I don't think . . .": Haskins, "Barbie's Little Secret."

"The promotion of dolls . . .": Winterman, "What Would a Real Life Barbie Look Like?"

"I don't think the concerns . . .": Ravitz, "50-Year-Old Barbie, Based on 'Gag Toy for Men.'"

"Barbie is far too . . ." and "They have fun with . . .": O'Hagan, "Toying with Perfection."

"The first time I saw . . .": E-mail to author.

"Perfect hair. Shapely . . .": Rogers, *Barbie Culture*, 17.

"some young girls see . . ." and "a lot more sway . . .": Clark-Flory, "Should parents ban Barbie?"

"Barbie was never viewed . . ." and "We also colored her hair . . .": E-mail to author.

"It's empowering for women . . .": Winterman, "What Would a Real Life Barbie Look Like?"

"She has long legs . . .": Cooke, "Not Looking Bad for 40, Barbie."

"plain and unpopular . . .": Ravitz, "50-Year-Old Barbie, Based on 'Gag Toy for Men.'"

"was breathtaking. And everyone . . .": Leung, "Becoming Barbie: Living Dolls."

"It was powerful," and "I thought . . .": Ravitz, "50-Year-Old Barbie, Based on 'Gag Toy for Men.'"

"perception problem . . ." and "It's not that . . .": Leung, "Becoming Barbie: Living Dolls."

"more reflective of . . .": Randolph, "Living Dolls."

"The fashions teens wear . . .": Jervis, "Barbie's New Bod, BFD."

"I think overreacting to . . .": Lord, *Forever Barbie*, 234.

"I do not believe . . .": Handler, *The Body Burden*, 12.

"Dolls often give . . .": Edut, *Body Outlaws*, 19.

"I think that Barbie, . . .": Molad, "American Icons: Barbie."

"The harm of these images . . ." Wolf, *The Beauty Myth*, 200.

CHAPTER 6

"Brother and Sister dolls . . .": Lord, *Forever Barbie*, 167.

"a doll with authentic . . .": Lord, *Forever Barbie*, 160.

"a daring, big step . . .": Mandeville, "Black Barbie."

"You don't know how . . .": Lord, *Forever Barbie*, 178.

"No longer did a young black . . .": Mandeville, "Black Barbie."

"My first black Barbie . . .": Raynor, "My First Black Barbie: Transforming the Image."

"I had very few dolls . . .": E-mail to author.

"ugly and bad": Lord, *Forever Barbie*, 164.

"asked us, 'What can . . .'": Hofmann, "Style Makers: Derek Hopson and Darlene Powell-Hopson, Child and Family Psychologists."

"Although Barbie has had . . .": Rogers, *Barbie Culture*, 47.

"Now, ethnic Barbie . . .": Berkwitz, "Finally, Barbie Doll Ads Go Ethnic."

"Regardless of what color dyes . . .": duCille, "Dyes and Dolls."

"Why [does Mattel] make . . .": Pekarik, "Understanding Visitor Comments."

"must be part" "is, like, Puerto Rican . . ." and "girls' dolls had beads . . .": Chin, "Ethnically Correct Dolls: Toying with the Race Industry."

"I used to have a lot . . .": Davis, *A Girl Like Me*.

"We added more . . .": duCille, "Dyes and Dolls."

"The hair, that hair, I want it . . .": duCille, *Skin Trade*, 51.

"We urban, Jewish, black . . ." and "I'd like to think that . . .": Edut, *Body Outlaws*, 17.

"represent the exquisite . . .": Raynor, "My First Black Barbie: Transforming the Image."

"In addition to her beauty . . ." and "She is beautiful . . .": Fisher, "AKAs Welcome Sister Barbie."

"She looks like a . . .": Lord, *Forever Barbie*, 177.

"The huasa costume was . . .": E-mail to author.

"I was insulted. . . ." "For many in . . ." "I like it . . ." and "She has a Puerto Rican . . .": Navarro, "A New Barbie in Puerto Rico Divides Island and Mainland."

"I've always hated Barbie . . .": E-mail to author.

"Why are we always pushing . . ." and "I want them to see . . .": "Mattel Introduces Black Barbies, to Mixed Reviews," *USA Today*.

CHAPTER 7

"neither with underpants or . . .": duCille, *Skin Trade*, 23.

"draw on the parts . . .": Conversation with the author.

"Barbie was never about . . .": Hamill, "A Grown-Up Barbie."

"My friends and I were not . . .": McDonough, *The Barbie Chronicles*, 53.

"He often mimicked adult roles . . .": Thomas, *Naked Barbies, Warrior Joes, and Other Forms of Visible Gender*, 135.

"Of course, you wouldn't want . . ." and "I had the twin-size . . .": Thomas, *Naked Barbies, Warrior Joes, and Other Forms of Visible Gender*, 144.

"My older neighbor had . . .": E-mail to author.

"My neighbor and I always had . . .": E-mail to author.

"How did I—the daughter of . . .": Haskins, "Barbie's Little Secret."

"I got my first . . .": E-mail to author.

"The Barbie Dream House had . . .": E-mail to author.

"Our naked Barbie collection . . .": E-mail to author.

"My brother used to torture . . ." "When I was little . . ." and "Barbie is a stupid . . .": Rogers, *Barbie Culture*, 31.

"When I was young . . .": E-mail to author.

"I am a boy so I don't . . .": E-mail to author.

"I'm a high-school senior . . .": E-mail to author.

"When I was a kid . . .": E-mail to author.

"Every little girl mutilates . . .": E-mail to author.

"She's just too unreal. . . .": Morrison, "Barbie Must Die."

"Messing with Barbie . . .": O'Hagan, "Toying with Perfection."

"My friend and I were at . . .": E-mail to author.

"When I was about eight . . .": E-mail to author.

"Let's just put it out there. . . .": E-mail to author.

"Is it not a cherished part . . .": Goldstein, "Should Barbie Die?"

"The idea of dressing . . .": E-mail to author.

"an 'incident' at school . . .": duCille, "Dyes and Dolls."

"I asked for Barbie dolls, . . .": E-mail to author.

"Barbie may look like . . .": O'Hagan, "Toying with Perfection."

"The doll provoked . . ." and "The most readily expressed . . .": "'Babyish' Barbie under Attack from Little Girls, Study Shows," University of Bath.

"a go at . . ." and "Send her to her . . .": Morrison, "Barbie Must Die."

"I knew a lot of people . . .": "Ditch the Doll?" MSNBC.com

"Have we all forgotten . . .": Treneman, "Time to Stop Hating Barbie."

CHAPTER 8

"Anytime you've got . . .": Molad, "American Icons: Barbie."

"For as much as I've heard . . .": E-mail to author.

"Dear Barbie, I can . . .": E-mail to author.

"I'm convinced I became . . ." and "It would be . . .": Kahn, "Forever Young."

"The parties are advised . . ." and "The beauty of Barbie . . .": Elliott, "Years Later, Mattel Embraces 'Barbie Girl.'"

"Life in Plastic . . .": Rasted, Søren, Claus Noréen, and René Dif, "Barbie Girl."

"one of the greatest . . ." and "It hit me that . . .": Brooks, "First Person Artist."

"Painted by Warhol . . .": Kahn, "A Onetime Bimbo Becomes a Muse."

"The concept of altering . . ." "I spend my time . . ." "Sometimes I try . . ." and "represents the good and the bad . . .": Cadelago, "The Sixth Annual Altered Barbie Art Show."

"Barbie has to be the . . ." and "I was always forced . . .": Yoe, *The Art of Barbie*, 8, 9.

"I put the doll . . .": Molad, "American Icons: Barbie."

"There was the stupid . . .": Wapshott, "Burn, Barbie, Burn: Reportage."

"Rather than trying . . ." and "She has acne . . .": Colotti, E-mail to author.

"a childhood spent . . .": Lange, e-mail to author.

"love-hate relationship: . . .": Walker," "Deconstructing Barbie."

"I don't believe it's fair . . ." and "Some people have a hard . . .": E-mail to author.

"My obsession with Barbie . . .": E-mail to author.

"The show with [Barbie's] paintings . . .": Vander Broek and Noer, "Barbie Turns 50."

CHAPTER 9

"I have you till you're . . .": Lord, *Forever Barbie*, 138.

"Never has a doll . . .": Treneman, "Time to Stop Hating Barbie."

"She is hardly going . . .": Treneman, "Time to Stop Hating Barbie."

"All hell broke loose. . . .": Gerber, *Barbie and Ruth*, 187.

"It was a very demeaning, . . .": Gerber, *Barbie and Ruth*, 190.

"It was heartbreaking. . . .": Gerber, *Barbie and Ruth*, 196.

"She always denied it . . ." and "There's no way a woman . . .": Klein, "Happy Birthday, Barbie."

"I was unable to . . .": Gerber, *Barbie and Ruth*, 169.

"I'm going into the breast . . .": Gerber, *Barbie and Ruth*, 200.

"I have a pink Barbie T-shirt . . .": E-mail to author.

"To take a woman who . . .": Gerber, *Barbie and Ruth*, 209-210.

"Both of us decided . . .": Gerber, *Barbie and Ruth*, 251.

"Barbie is bigger than . . .": Lord, *Forever Barbie*, 80.

Bibliography

✳

Amerman, John W. *The Story of Mattel, Inc.: Fifty Years of Innovation*. New York: The Newcomen Society of the United States, 1995.

"'Babyish' Barbie Under Attack from Little Girls, Study Shows." University of Bath, press release for Agnes Nairn, December 19, 2005.

Baker, Kenneth. "Toy Soldiers, Plastic Cowboys, Barbie Dolls—What Could Be More Simple and Innocent? Well, They're Not When Photographer David Levinthal Gets Through with Them." *San Francisco Chronicle*, April 15, 2006.

"Barbie Girls Play Rough." BBC News, February 14, 2009.

"Barbie Turns 50." NPR Radio: *On Point with Tom Ashbrook*, February 12, 2009.

Berkwitz, David N. "Finally, Barbie Doll Ads Go Ethnic." *Newsweek*. August 13, 1990.

BillyBoy. *Barbie: Her Life and Times*. New York: Crown, 1987.

Brett, Jennifer. "Barbie's the Birthday Doll: Iconic Doll Mirrors Society Throughout the Decades, With a Multi-faceted Career, Clothes, Accessories Galore." *The Atlanta Journal-Constitution*, March 9, 2009.

Brooks, Kimberly. "First Person Artist: Barbie as the Ultimate Muse." *The Huffington Post*, January 18, 2008.

Brumberg, Joan Jacobs. *The Body Project: An Intimate History of American Girls*. New York: Random House, 1998.

Cadelago, Chris. "The Sixth Annual Altered Barbie Art Show." *San Francisco Chronicle*, August 3, 2008.

Chamberlain, Kathy. "Idollatry." *Tikkun*. March–April, 1995.

Champion Media. Radio broadcast, May 17, 2009. www.championmediaonline.com.

Chin, Elizabeth. "Ethnically Correct Dolls: Toying with the Race Industry." *American Anthropologist*. New Series, vol. 101, no. 2 (June 1999), pp. 305–321.

Clark, Eric. *The Real Toy Story: Inside the Ruthless Battle for America's Youngest Consumers*. New York: Free Press, 2007.

Clark, Kenneth B., and Clark, Mamie Phipps. "Racial Identification and Preference in Negro Children." *Readings in Social Psychology*, pp. 169–178. New York: Henry Holt, 1947.

Clark-Flory, Tracy. "Should Parents Ban Barbie?" Salon.com, January 10, 2009.

Cooke, Angela. "Not Looking Bad for 40, Barbie." *Sunday Mirror*. January 17, 1999.

Cross, Gary. *Kids' Stuff: Toys and the Changing World of American Childhood*. Cambridge, Mass.: Harvard University Press, 1997.

Davis, Kiri. *A Girl Like Me*. New York: Reel Works Teen Filmmaking, 2005. Film.

"Ditch the Doll? Lawmaker Out to Outlaw Barbie." MSNBC.com, March 4, 2009.

duCille, Ann. "Dyes and Dolls: Multicultural Barbie and the Merchandising of Difference." *Journal of Feminist Cultural Studies*, Spring 1994.

duCille, Ann. *Skin Trade*. Cambridge, Mass.: Harvard University Press, 1996.

Duffy, Judith. "Barbie's Figure 'Gives Young Girls a Desire to Have a Thinner Body.'" *The Sunday Herald*. June 12, 2005.

Ebersole, Lucinda, and Richard Peabody. *Mondo Barbie: An Anthology of Fiction and Poetry*. New York: St. Martin's Press, 1993.

Ebrahimzadeh, Parissa. "Syrian Barbie." *Forbes*, March 5, 2009.

Edut, Ophira. *Body Outlaws: Young Women Write About Body Image and Identity*. Seattle, Wash.: Seal Press, 2000.

Elliott, Stuart. "Years Later, Mattel Embraces 'Barbie Girl.'" *New York Times*, August 26, 2009.

Farnham, Alan. *Forbes Great Success Stories: Twelve Tales of Victory Wrested from Defeat*. New York: John Wiley & Sons, 2000.

"Fashion: Black Look in Beauty." *Time*, April 11, 1969.

"Feminists Protest 'Sexist' Toys in Fair." *New York Times*. February 29, 1972.

Firestone, David. "While Barbie Talks Tough, G.I. Joe Goes Shopping." *New York Times*, December 31, 1993.

Fisher, Harold T. "AKAs Welcome Sister Barbie." *The Baltimore Sun*. October 12, 2008.

Fishkoff, Sue. "A Jewish Girl in a Barbie World." *Jerusalem Post*, May 27, 2006.

Frean, Alexandra. "Barbarism Begins with Barbie, the Doll Children Love to Hate." *Times Online* (London), December 19, 2005.

Friedan, Betty. *The Feminist Mystique*. Introduction by Anna Quindlen. New York: W. W. Norton & Company, 2001.

Gerber, Robin. *Barbie and Ruth: The Story of the World's Most Famous Doll and the Woman Who Created Her*. New York: HarperCollins, 2009.

Goff, Keli. "Appreciation: Naomi Sims, the First Black Supermodel." *Time*, August 5, 2009.

Goldstein, Sarah. "Should Barbie Die? Before You Destroy Her, Think of Your Life Without Her." Salon.com, June 22, 2006.

Green, Michelle, and Denise Gellene. "As a Tiny Plastic Star Turns 30, the Real Barbie and Ken Reflect on Life in the Shadow of the Dolls." *People*, March 6, 1989.

Grewal, Inderpal. *Transnational America: Feminisms, Diasporas, Neoliberalisms*. Durham, N.C.: Duke University Press, 2005.

Hamill, Jane. "A Grown-Up Barbie." NPR, "Morning Edition," May 22, 2006.

Handler, Elliot. *The Impossible Really Is Possible: The Story of Mattel*. New York: The Newcomen Society of the United States, 1968.

Handler, Ruth, with Jacqueline Shannon. *Dream Doll: The Ruth Handler Story*. Stamford, Conn.: Longmeadow Press, 1994.

Handler, Stacey. *The Body Burden: Living in the Shadow of Barbie*. Cape Canaveral, Fla.: Blue Note Publications, 2000.

Haskins, Sarah. "Barbie's Little Secret." *The Washington Post*, March 8, 2009.

Hofmann, Deborah. "Style Makers: Derek Hopson and Darlene Powell-Hopson, Child and Family Psychologists." *New York Times*. March 17, 1991.

Jehl, Douglas. "Cairo Journal: It's Barbie vs. Laila and Sara in Mideast Culture War." *New York Times*, June 2, 1999.

Jervis, Lisa. "Barbie's New Bod, BFD." *Mother Jones*, December 4, 1997.

Jones, Abby, and Sara Newman. "Hello, Dolly! Is the Barbie Image Hurting Your Body Image?" *New Moon*, September–October 2007.

Kahn, Alice. "A Onetime Bimbo Becomes a Muse." *New York Times*, September 29, 1991.

Kahn, Joseph P. "Forever Young." *Boston Globe*, March 5, 2009.

Kauffman, Hattie. "Birthday Girl Barbie." CBS News: *The Early Show*, March 9, 2009.

Kershaw, Sarah. "Ruth Handler, Whose Barbie Gave Dolls Curves, Dies at 85." *New York Times*, April 29, 2002.

Klein, Julia. "Happy Birthday, Barbie." *AARP Bulletin Today*, March 9, 2009.

Koss, Amy Goldman. "My Barbie." *Los Angeles Times*, March 9, 2009.

Kuther, Tara L. and Erin McDonald. "Early Adolescents' Experiences with, and Views of, Barbie." *Adolescence*, Spring 2004.

La Ferla, Ruth. "Losing the Limo: New Fashion Dolls." *New York Times*, November 6, 2009.

Lee, Carol E. "The Evolution of Women's Roles, Chronicled in the Life of a Doll." *New York Times*, March 30, 2004.

Lefkof, Amy. "Barbie (and Ken) Raised My Consciousness." *New York Times*, Op-Ed, September 16, 1994.

Leung, Rebecca. "Becoming Barbie: Living Dolls." CBSNews.com, August 6, 2004.

Lord, M. G. *Forever Barbie*. New York: Walker & Company, 2004.

Loughrey, Felicity. "Hello Dolly." *Vogue* (Australia), April 9, 2009, pp. 192–197.

Mandeville, A. Glenn. "Black Barbie." *Barbie Bazaar*, May/June 1996, pp. 25–29.

Marsh, Jackie, ed. *Popular Culture, New Media and Digital Literacy in Early Childhood*. New York: RoutledgeFalmer, 2005.

Martin, Courtney E. *Perfect Girls, Starving Daughters: How the Quest for Perfection Is Harming Young Women*. New York: Berkley Books, 2007.

Marwick, Arthur. *The Sixties: Cultural Revolution in Britain, France, Italy, and the United States c. 1958–c. 1974*. Oxford, England: Oxford University Press, 1998.

"Mattel Hopes Shanghai Is a Barbie World." NPR, *Morning Edition*, March 6, 2009.

"Mattel Introduces Black Barbies, to Mixed Reviews." *USA Today*, October 29, 2009.

"Mattel Says It Erred: Teen Talk Barbie Turns Silent on Math." *New York Times*, October 21, 1992.

McDonough, Yona Zeldis. *The Barbie Chronicles*. New York: Simon and Schuster/Touchstone, 1999.

Messner, Michael A. *Out of Play: Critical Essays on Gender and Sport*. Albany, N.Y.: State University of New York Press, 2007.

Miller, Claire Cain. "Barbies's Next Career? Computer Engineer." *New York Times*, February 12, 2010.

Miller, G. Wayne. *Toy Wars: The Epic Struggle Between G.I. Joe, Barbie, and the Companies That Make Them*. New York: Random House, 1998.

"Modern Living: Black Cosmetics." *Time*, June 29, 1970.

Molad, Leital. "American Icons: Barbie." *Studio 360*, March 31, 2006.

Morrison, Patt. "Barbie Must Die." *Los Angeles Times*, June 22, 2006.

Nadrich, Garett R. "Court Backs Barbie Artist in Doll of a Case." Fox News.com, August 15, 2001.

Navarro, Mireya. "A New Barbie in Puerto Rico Divides Island and Mainland." *New York Times*, December 27, 1997.

O'Brien, Richard. *The Story of American Toys: From the Puritans to the Present*. New York: Abbeville Press, 1990.

O'Hagan, Anne. "Toying with Perfection." *Chatelaine*, March 2009.

Oppenheimer, Jerry. *Toy Monster: The Big, Bad World of Mattel*. New York: John Wiley & Sons, 2009.

Orecklin, Michele. "The Role of Race." *Time*, August 28, 2003.

Page, Clarence. "A Doll for All." *The News Hour with Jim Lehrer*, February 26, 1998.

Peers, Juliette. *The Fashion Doll: From Bebe Jumeau to Barbie*. New York: Berg Publishers, 2004.

Pekarik, A. J. "Understanding Visitor Comments: The Case of Flight Time Barbie." *Curator: The Museum Journal*, Vol. 40, no. 1 (1997), pp. 56–68.

Phelan, James. *Living to Tell About It: A Rhetoric and Ethics of Character Narration*. Ithaca, N.Y.: Cornell University Press, 2005.

Phelan, Sara. "Feminists and Fans Both Ask: 'Will the Real Barbie Step Forward?'" *Metro Santa Cruz*, March 13–19, 1997.

Quindlen, Anna. "Public & Private; Barbie at 35." *New York Times*, September 10, 1994.

Rand, Erica. *Barbie's Queer Accessories*. Durham, N.C.: Duke University Press, 1995.

Randolph, Laura B. "Living Dolls." *Ebony*, January 1998.

Ravitz, Jessica. "50-Year-Old Barbie, Based on 'Gag Toy for Men.'" CNN.com, March 9, 2009.

Raynor, Sharon. "My First Black Barbie: Transforming the Image." *Cultural Studies, Critical Methodologies*, April 2009, pp. 179–185.

Robins, Cynthia. *Barbie: Thirty Years of America's Doll*. New York: Contemporary Books, 1989.

Rogers, Mary F. *Barbie Culture*. London: Sage Publications, 1999.

Rosenberg, Tina. "Editorial Observer; The New Age Barbie Is an Old-Fashioned Doll." *New York Times*, November 30, 1997.

Steele, Valerie. *Art, Design, and Barbie: The Evolution of a Cultural Icon*. New York: Exhibitions International, 1995.

Steinberg, Neil. "You Always Hurt the Ones You Love." *Forbes*, March 5, 2009.

Stern, Susan. *Barbie Nation: An Unauthorized Tour*, DVD. Directed by Susan Stern. San Francisco: El Rio Productions, 2003.

Stern, Sydney Ladensohn, and Ted Schoenhaus. *Toyland: The High-Stakes Game of the Toy Industry*. Chicago: Contemporary Books, 1990.

Thomas, Jeannie Banks. *Naked Barbies, Warrior Joes, and Other Forms of Visible Gender*. Chicago: University of Illinois Press, 2003.

"Through Her 50 Years on Toy-Store Shelves, Barbie, the Ectomorphic Doll Who Goes Hollywood Starlets One Better by Being Made Entirely of Plastic." *National Review*, April 6, 2009.

Treneman, Ann. "Time to Stop Hating Barbie." *The Independent*, March 8, 1999.

Vander Broek, Anna, and Noer, Michael. "Barbie Turns 50." *Forbes*, March 5, 2009.

Walker, Rob. "Deconstructing Barbie." *New York Times*, January 25, 2009.

Wapshott, Nicholas. "Burn, Barbie, Burn: Reportage." *The Times*, June 30, 2004.

Westenhouser, Kitturah B. *The Story of Barbie*. Paducah, Ky.: Collector Books, 1994.

Winterman, Denise. "What Would a Real Life Barbie Look Like?" *BBC News Magazine*, March 6, 2009.

Wolf, Naomi. *The Beauty Myth*. New York: HarperCollins, 2002.

Yoe, Craig. *The Art of Barbie: Artists Celebrate the World's Favorite Doll*. New York: Workman Publishing, 1994.

Zoepf, Katherine. "Bestseller in Mideast: Barbie with a Prayer Mat." *New York Times*, September 22, 2005.

Photo Credits

✻

Note: All of the photographs by Karen Pike Photography feature Peter Harrigan's fabulous Barbie collection, which consists mostly of reproductions of vintage dolls, as well as many contemporary dolls.

Half title page, title page, pages 1, 4, 7, 8: © Karen Pike Photography

Page 12: Schlesinger Library, Radcliffe Institute, Harvard University

Page 16: Image courtesy of Ellen and Ned Solway, Deja-voodoo.com

Page 18: Schlesinger Library, Radcliffe Institute, Harvard University

Page 20: Everett Collection

Page 24: (top) Dolls courtesy of Lorette Sousie/© Karen Pike Photography; (bottom and background) Paper doll/clothes by DeJournette Co./Image courtesy of Paperdoll Review

Pages 25, 26: Everett Collection

Page 27: Doll from the collection of dal Lowenbein/Photo by dal Lowenbein

Pages 29, 30, 34–37, 40: © Karen Pike Photography

Page 43 (top) Photo by Eric Long, National Air and Space Museum, Smithsonian Institution (SI 2009-30460; (right) © Karen Pike Photography

Pages 44–46, 48–49: © Karen Pike Photography

Page 50: Photo by Santi Visalli Inc./Archive Photos/Getty Images

Pages 53, 55, 57, 59: © Karen Pike Photography

Page 60: Photo by Dave M. Benett/Getty Images

Page 61: © Karen Pike Photography

Page 64: (left) Photo by Yale Joel/Time & Life Pictures/Getty Images; (right) © Karen Pike Photography

Pages 65, 67, 69–73, 75–81: © Karen Pike Photography

Page 82: (top) Image Courtesy of Emily Cohen, (middle) Photo © Margaux Lange, (bottom) Courtesy of Deborah Colotti

Page 84: Photo courtesy of James Valastro

Pages 85–87, 90–91: © Karen Pike Photography

Page 95: Still from the motion picture "The Tribe"/Art Director Gil Gershoni

Page 97: (left) Courtesy of Deborah Colotti; (right) AFP/AFP/Getty Images

Page 98: (left) © David Rosenzweig; (right) Photo by Mark Van Amburgh, QuadPhoto-Saratoga © Quad Graphics/Courtesy of Margaux Lange

Page 100: Photo by DMI/DMI/Time & Life Pictures/Getty Images

Pages 102–103: © Karen Pike Photography

Page 105: (top) Photo by Allan Grant/Time Life Pictures/Getty Images; (bottom) MATT CAMPBELL/AFP/Getty Images

Page 107: (top) LEE CELANO/AFP/Getty Images; (bottom) © Karen Pike Photography

Page 108: © Karen Pike Photography

INDEX

✳

"We made her quite bland. . . . We never mad[e]

*"I NEVER HAD a problem with what she lo[oks]
wasn't real. Why would I compare myself to a[

from now, when archaeologists uncover the cities and
Barbie dolls, they will identify her as the fertility godd[ess]

no messages; it was we who gave Barbie me[

Barbie like a baby doll; they boss her around

destructive force on the self-image of women all over the glob[e]

A MONSTER, SHE IS OUR MONSTER."—Ann[a

University * "Barbie . . . seemed to demand a sta[
over, because more than Barbie was at stake."—

MADE BARBIE, literally and figuratively. Sh[e
about to change radically."—BillyBoy, fashion designe[r

from their dolls but from the women around them. Most
ful female role model in my life. . . . She had the good s[

—Yona Zeldis McDonough, author of The Barbie Chronicles * "I
that the only thing that's important is being tall a[

—Anna Quindlen, journalist * "Her teeth were blackened, and
represented, and that's why I liked her best."—Julie, age 19[

generation of 'Barbie girls' is now entering the world and we se[

as recognizable as the Coke bottle."—Patt Morris[on